"This book is fascinating reading, especially if one has read one of the books written by Japanese businessmen who have been successful in building great companies. The Korean views of what lies behind the success of Daewoo are quite different from what would be said in a similar Japanese book."

—LESTER THUROW
Dean, Sloan School of Management,
Massachusetts Institute of Technology,
and author of *Head to Head*

"In Korea they spell Horatio Alger, Kim Woo-Choong."

—CHRISTOPHER FORBES
Vice chairman of *Forbes* magazine

"Chairman Kim Woo-Choong is a courageous and legendary entrepreneur. Students and practitioners of free enterprise will benefit greatly from a study of the history of Chairman Kim's successes to date and the legacy he has built."

—ALEXANDER M. HAIG, JR.
Former secretary of state and
former president of
United Technologies

EVERY
STREET IS
PAVED WITH
GOLD

EVERY STREET IS PAVED WITH GOLD

The Road to Real Success

KIM WOO-CHOONG

INTRODUCTION BY LOUIS KRAAR

WILLIAM MORROW AND COMPANY, INC.
NEW YORK

Many chapters of this book were previously published in slightly different form by Times Books International in Singapore as *Every Street Is Paved with Gold: Success Secrets of an Asian Entrepreneur,* copyright © 1992 by Times Editions Pte Ltd.

This previously published material is a translation of *Se-Gye-Neun Nulb-Go Hal-Il-Eun Man-Ta,* published by Gimm-Young Company, Publisher, copyright © 1989.

It is the policy of William Morrow and Company, Inc., and its imprints and affiliates, recognizing the importance of preserving what has been written, to print the books we publish on acid-free paper, and we exert our best efforts to that end.

Library of Congress Cataloging-in-Publication Data
Kim, U-jung
    Every street is paved with gold: the road to real success / by Woo-Choong Kim ; introduction by Louis Kraar
        p. cm.
    ISBN 0-688-11327-3
    1. Success in business—Korea (South)   2. Taeu Group.
3. Industrial management—Korea (South)   4. Kim, U-jung.
HF5386.K484   1992
650.1—dc20   92-266
                                                                 CIP

Printed in the United States of America

First Edition

1 2 3 4 5 6 7 8 9 10

BOOK DESIGN BY BARBARA COHEN ARONICA

To all those who have been part
of the Daewoo family
during the past twenty-five years

My sincere thanks to Louis Kraar for his invaluable help in the expansion and adaptation of my original Korean book for this English-language edition.

Contents

Introduction

BY LOUIS KRAAR

Starting with nothing after the devastating Korean War, Kim Woo-Choong built one of the world's largest corporations. The founder and chairman of Daewoo, Kim personifies the drive and imagination that makes East Asia a dynamic center of economic growth. He thrives at home by taking over troubled companies and revitalizing them. The ultimate international entrepreneur, Kim finds profits even in such forbidding markets as Iran. His relentless drive has created a group of twenty-two main companies that cover a spectrum from heavy industry and electronics to pianos and hotels. As Chairman Kim puts it, "I can smell money every-where."

A restless, professorial-looking man of fifty-five, Kim has almost boundless global reach. He spends over half of every year roaming the world to sniff out opportunities. He ships

Korean cars to Czechoslovakia, produces videocassette record-
ers in Northern Ireland, and owns a designer of microchips in
California's Silicon Valley. Kim may not be a household word
yet in the West, but Americans are surrounded by his products: Pontiac LeMans autos, Caterpillar forklifts, sections of
Boeing jetliners, and Leading Edge computers. No wonder
that in 1991 his Daewoo group rang up sales of $25 billion—
more than Xerox, Eastman Kodak, or RJR Nabisco.

Kim shows why economic power is shifting from the West
to Asia in ways that benefit practically all nations. He is an
Asian equivalent of Andrew Carnegie or John D. Rockefeller,
but with a distinctive spirit of ingenuity and self-sacrifice. Everyone can learn a lot from Kim, especially his extraordinary
skills in motivating people. And his adventurous life makes the
original Horatio Alger seem almost wimpish.

This book by Kim, a best-seller in the Korean language,
was originally a collection of short essays addressed to the
youth of his country—but with a universal message. It has been
expanded and adapted. In South Korea, Kim has sparked a
popular response similar to that ignited in the United States by
the pithy books of Lee Iacocca, chairman of Chrysler Corporation. Kim's wisdom is sterner stuff. He finds work more exciting than play and hates to see money wasted on the pursuit of
pleasure. His neo-Confucian views, however, are a key to the
rise of South Korea as an industrial powerhouse—and to the
outstanding performance of other East Asian economies.

One of the elements that make Kim's book far more than
just morality lectures by a highly successful businessman is his
own saga. And Kim has a gift for converting problems into
opportunities. Forced to spend the spring of 1989 settling a

strike at the Daewoo shipyard in Okpo on the southern island of Koje, Kim used the long nights to write this book.

A daring risk-taker in the Third World, Kim has snared over $10 billion in civilian construction contracts in Libya. He started building railway lines in Iran during the height of its war with Iraq. Kim does not regard those efforts as reckless. As he puts it: "If you're going into a risky place, you pay more attention to everything, so actually there's no risk." Moreover, he only picks projects that have clear benefits to the people of the country, projects likely to survive a radical change of regime. Whether a new government would continue any given project is both a moral test for Kim and an economic one.

Kim is certainly driven, though not by greed. Having built the forty-fifth-largest corporation on earth, Kim has made a fortune—and given most of it away to foundations for medical care, research in basic science, and education. As he once said, "I don't care about money-making because I could do that anytime." Instead, Kim professes to have been inspired partly by the need to create a big business that would help lift South Korea out of poverty. In his book, Kim is practically lyrical about the satisfaction of accomplishment, saying that "I haven't worked like a madman just to make a few coins" and describing "the joy of doing what everyone said was impossible."

Kim occupies a unique position in the Korean business world. Like Hyundai and Samsung, Kim's company is one of the large conglomerates called *chaebol,* which initially flourished on huge injections of government credit and now dominate South Korea's economy. Still, Kim is different. He is the youngest and only college-educated founder of a Korean corporate giant. He spurns the common Korean practice of using his companies to build a super-rich family dynasty. Says Kim: "Daewoo is not something I can or will pass on to my family. I hope to be evaluated as a businessman who knew the differences between ownership and leadership."

At times he seems almost too good to be real. Kim, however, comes from what he describes as "a generation of sacrifice" tempered by unusual hardships. He was born into a country torn apart by turmoil—harshly occupied by Japan for thirty-five years until 1945, then thrust into the Korean War, which partitioned the nation and, as Kim notes, "destroyed what little industry we had." In the wake of that wreckage, the West tended to write off South Korea as hopeless. Kim helped prove that the assessment was ridiculous. When he graduated from college, the country's average income per person was a mere $76 a year—and now it's over $6,000. Kim has moved from manufacturing textiles to shipbuilding and autos in the seventies, to electronics in the eighties, and is going into aerospace products for the nineties.

Rather than running a one-man show, Kim has multiplied his effectiveness by infusing some 90,000 employees with his aggressive and creative spirit. Dr. Park Sung-Kyou, president of Daewoo Telecom, left a promising career in the United States more than a decade ago to return to his homeland because of Kim. Says Park: "The chairman appeals to patriotism and Confucianism—and he gives executives considerable autonomy."

Kim's exploits have won recognition at home and abroad. In June 1984, Sweden's King Carl XVI Gustaf presented Kim with the International Business Award, given every three years by the International Chamber of Commerce to honor "an entrepreneur who has contributed to the idea of free enterprise by either creating or developing his own company." In 1988 an opinion poll by the Korean magazine *Economist* selected Kim as the most respected businessman in his country. The following year the Seoul office of UNESCO named Kim as its man of the year for his contribution to the economy and dedication to work. He has been decorated by the governments of Pakistan and Sudan for contributing to their economic development, awarded honorary degrees in the United States and Korea, and picked by women college students in his own country as the most trust-inspiring Korean businessman.

Kim acknowledges personal shortcomings. "I don't know music or painting. I suppose that's unbalanced, but my full attention goes to business." Outsiders spot other possible blemishes. Competitors in Korea regard Kim as an aggressive high roller—as one rival puts it, "dominated by the almost reckless drive for nearly any business opportunities." Some bankers fret about the risks that he takes in volatile Third World countries, including work for the unpredictable regime of Libya's Colonel Muammar Qaddafi. Westerners have wondered how long Kim could push employees to work long hours for relatively low pay.

Though Korean wages have risen sharply in recent years, Kim has an increasingly tough time persuading workers to share his notions of self-sacrifice. His book is part of a broader effort that helps Kim to prevail over unprecedented challenges. The cheap, submissive labor force on which Kim built his initial success has faded with the nation's prosperity. Ever since South Korea shifted toward democratic government in mid-1987, unions have frequently staged long strikes for higher pay.

In just the past several years, Korea's manufacturing wages have doubled to over $650 monthly, much higher than in such other ambitious Asian countries as Thailand and the Philippines. Simultaneously, the Korean *won* has appreciated against the U.S. dollar—straining the international competitiveness that is Kim's great advantage.

Moreover, Korean business leaders who have long been hailed at home as heroes of Korea's economic advancement are now widely accused of being Oriental robber barons. Politicians complain about an unhealthy concentration of influence and wealth: founding families manage most Korean conglomerates and own about half of their total assets. Kim, who donated most of his personal shares in Daewoo to charitable foundations long before this furor, says: "Nowadays everyone complains because most of the profit goes into the big owner's pocket." The Korean government is pushing other companies to go public, as Daewoo voluntarily did years ago.

Kim's zeal for work has made him a cult figure among colleagues, who still often refer to him as *tosa,* or master— meaning a kung fu teacher who shows followers how to jump higher than they thought possible. From the start, his idea of leadership included keeping commitments to customers, even if someone had to fly in with cloth from Japan and an order was filled at a loss.

By sheer persistence, Kim broke into supplying garments to large U.S. retailers in the seventies. He purchased American shirts in every size, then had them taken apart stitch by stitch to copy. Daewoo set up a sales office in New York, where Kim often knocked on doors of potential customers without an appointment. He says, "Instead of seeing three or four customers a day, I could see ten." He overcame the reluctance of the giant American retail chain Sears by setting up a replica of its U.S. garment-testing facilities in Korea. When the United States and Europe put quotas on garment imports, Kim's company cornered much of Korea's allotment—and cleaned up. He did that by tuning in to information—one of his most effective business techniques. On his first visit to the United States in 1970, he heard about possible import restrictions and shrewdly prepared for them. Allocation of quotas was based on past performance, so Daewoo got nearly 40 percent of the total for Korea and became highly profitable.

Kim swiftly diversified Daewoo by entering businesses with the fewest competitors. He went from exporting textiles to making them, then acquired factories for producing handbags and gloves. He found that other big Korean companies were not engaged in financial services, so Daewoo invested in banks, finance companies, and insurance firms. From the start, he expanded by buying troubled firms and reviving them. "I'm not a corporate raider," insists Kim. Instead of stripping assets and firing employees of the companies that he acquires, Kim pumps in capital and management expertise to save jobs. He sees ailing companies differently from most executives—focusing on the possibilities, rather than the difficulties.

As the broker James Capel points out in a recent study of Korean conglomerates, Chairman Kim's "judicious use of capital earned him the reputation of expertise in financial management, an attribute lacking at most other *chaebols*. . . . Kim Woo-Choong eventually embarked on a series of corporate acquisitions and takeovers, pushing Daewoo to the front line of Korean business combines."

Political connections helped Daewoo and other conglomerates grow. In 1976, Korea's late President Park Chung-Hee handed Kim his opportunity to buy into heavy industry—though at the time it didn't look like any great favor. President Park was a former student of Kim's father's at Taegu Normal School, which provided invaluable access for Daewoo, but no special privileges. The Park regime revved up the economy by providing low-interest credit to successful exporters. In short, the government backed businessmen who proved themselves to be winners. Kim was invited to take over a state-owned machinery plant that had been losing money for thirty-seven years and was heavily in debt.

The idea of taking on such a burden horrified most Daewoo executives, but Kim could not resist. He even temporarily broke his rule against employing relatives and persuaded his brother Kim Duk-Choong, an economist and university professor, to serve as Daewoo's chief executive for a while so that the chairman could focus on the machinery plant. Says economist Kim: "My brother was risking everything, so I had to help."

Chairman Kim worked, ate, and slept for several months at the factory of what is now Daewoo Heavy Industries. In nine months he began turning around the company. Kim says, "Never in my life have I worked so hard."

Living in the plant, Kim quickly discovered what was wrong. Production employees were putting in overtime because they couldn't survive on what they earned for eight-hour shifts, but they were not working hard. "The machinery was turning, but it wasn't producing anything," recalls Kim. He agreed to pay workers for twelve hours a day, but insisted that they earn the money. Kim also pumped several million dollars—half of the company's capital—into a modern cafeteria, barbershops, and housing for employees to raise their morale. He cut costs of components for German diesel engines made under license by purchasing in quantity and for cash. Before Daewoo took over the plant, it had been so unreliable that Korean truck makers had wangled government permits to import diesel engines. Kim produced ten thousand more engines than he had orders for, he says, "so truck makers would have no excuse to import engines."

His success with the heavy machinery plant established Kim's reputation as more than merely another shrewd trader. The takeover and turnaround of that company widened his ambitions—and changed the direction of Daewoo. As Kim says, "Had we not bought that firm, today we would not be producing forklift trucks for Caterpillar or making parts for Boeing aircraft."

Having proved himself as a company doctor, Kim persuaded the government to allow Daewoo to buy a Korean automaker with links to General Motors. Kim's Daewoo Motor, which was 50 percent owned by GM, makes the Pontiac LeMans for both the Korean and American markets. More important to Kim in the long run are four profitable joint ventures with GM that make various auto parts for export. Inside many GM models assembled elsewhere are components from Kim's factories. Eventually, Kim expects that exports of auto parts will be worth more than his shipments of entire cars.

Kim's global ambitions in the auto industry, however, have collided with the bureaucracy of GM, the world's largest auto manufacturer. Daewoo sales of cars to Czechoslovakia, for example, annoyed its partner in Detroit. GM insisted that its

German subsidiary supply Europe—creating stormy relations between Daewoo and the big American automaker. "There's a difference of philosophy," explains Kim. "The American way of thinking is to ask where is the market. We say that if we have the capacity and can produce competitively, then why can't we sell it?" Kim also complains that GM, which sells Korean-made cars through its dealers in the United States, has high overheads that inflate retail prices of the LeMans. Amid GM's sagging worldwide profits, the American company lost patience with Kim, with quality-control problems (now resolved), and with Korea's rising labor costs.

The differences between Kim and GM escalated into a classic clash between aggressive Asian zeal for growth of market share and American concern for shorter term profits. Finally, Kim resolved the conflict by simply divorcing the American automaker—buying out GM's half of Daewoo Motor. For all the bitterness, Kim managed to make the split friendly enough to continue supplying cars to the United States and to maintain the separate joint ventures that make GM car components.

Daewoo has some eighty offices scattered around the world. Kim flies into these countries to serve as his company's top salesman, as well as to soak up information from economists, businessmen, journalists, and government officials. Kim says that he wants "the feel and smell" of both hazards and opportunities. With firsthand information, he adds, "I can operate." In one new Third World market, Kim shocked his staff by scaling down their bid for a big construction project, calling the tactic "our admission fee." By sacrificing short-term profits on that job, Kim opened the way for much more business later.

In the same spirit, Kim has marched into China and Eastern Europe. He says: "We were limited to maybe half the markets in the world before because we had no trade with the socialist countries." Now Daewoo is producing refrigerators in southern China. Kim landed an agreement to export cars, electronic equipment, and other machinery to Hungary, where Daewoo has also set up a joint-venture investment bank. Kim has opened Daewoo offices in Moscow, Sofia, Warsaw, and Ho Chi Minh City.

Kim has been, in a sense, an unofficial ambassador, for his entry into markets has helped South Korea gain diplomatic relations with most of the countries in which he does business, including Algeria, Hungary, and the former Soviet Union. Already Kim has crossed another long-forbidden frontier, business with North Korea. A thaw in relations between South and North Korea gave Kim his opening. In January 1992, with permission from his government, Kim traveled to the communist North, which he terms "the world's last closed market," and made a deal to set up nine factories to make such things as shirts, running shoes, toys, and luggage. Kim figures that combining South Korea's capital and know-how with North Korea's cheap but disciplined labor could produce highly competitive export products. The Daewoo chairman also discovered that North Koreans knew all about him—because they had read his book.

At home, Kim's greatest challenge has been reviving a huge shipyard that he never wanted in the first place. In 1978 the Korean government asked him to take over the yard, which was only one-quarter completed and mired in debt. Kim refused, but the government simply waited until he was off on one of his trips abroad and announced the move anyway. Daewoo Shipbuilding, as it is now called, has tested even Kim's prowess. Before the yard's completion in 1981, Kim roamed the world to sell ships, initially without success. He decided on the daring strategy of building a technologically complex vessel to show what Daewoo could do. Kim sold a sophisticated stainless-steel chemical tanker to a Norwegian shipping company, which didn't have to take delivery if it was not satisfied. Kim made no profit, but the ship won awards for the outstanding vessel of 1982.

Hard selling, though, was not enough to rescue the shipyard. In 1982, Kim sold U.S. Lines a fleet of container ships, but the customer later ran into financial difficulties and could not pay. Worse, worldwide demand for ships slumped, and so did Daewoo Shipbuilding.

Now Kim is betting his reputation and $1.2 billion on turning around the troubled shipyard. With characteristic daring, he is diversifying Daewoo Shipbuilding into minicars, heavy trucks, and excavators. The Korean government, which owns 33 percent of the enterprise, is injecting half of the fresh capital via interest-free loans. The other half is coming from Kim, who has sold shares in his profitable stock brokerage firm and invested the proceeds in the shipyard. Kim has spent much of the past two years repairing labor relations at the shipyard on Koje island, where two employees died by self-immolation during a strike in the spring of 1989.

Kim has remarked that political and labor conflicts in Korea are really healthy. Everyone's complaints are being heard, and that will lead to consensus. As Kim put it, "Living standards here should go up. Our labor costs are still well below those in Japan and the United States. Productivity is what we have to think about." To offset higher wages, Kim is already automating factories, turning out diesel engines with robots designed by his own engineers. "I'm optimistic about the future," he says. In 1991, the shipyard turned a profit.

Kim, in fact, worries much more about the decline of American competitiveness than his own. He frets that the best and brightest Americans go into law and investment banking, while marketing and manufacturing get neglected. He is disturbed about reports in the American press on the effects of drug and alcohol abuse on U.S. factory workers. But he is impressed with what he sees as a revitalization of the American work ethic and a new spirit of progress.

(Though an admirer of the United States, Kim sounds a lot like Lee Iacocca in his criticisms of America. "The American company is not what it used to be," says Kim. "In the old days, Americans worked hard to challenge new frontiers. But as their economy got mature, they became more interested in nice houses, jogging, and having a good time than in doing business. How can you compete without dedication?"

Similarly, he worries that as Korea prospers its young will think the country has become as rich as America and will be more hedonistic. "It's a little premature for us to sit around feeling satisfied," says Kim.)

Besides sniffing out money everywhere, Kim is eager to fire up his countrymen with the brand of enthusiasm that keeps pushing him forward. He advises: "You have to find places that people have never been to, and you have to do things that people haven't done yet." He confesses to harboring another dream, to produce something in Korea, any product, that will be recognized as the finest in the world. Holding up a cigarette lighter, he remarks: "Instead of Dunhill, maybe everyone will use the Kim Woo-Choong." Those who know Kim assume that his dream product will be more substantial than a lighter and that it will become a reality eventually. As his book shows, Kim has already produced world-class advice for anyone who is ambitious enough to emulate his example.

Wherever I go, I immediately see where money is to be made. I once joked that every street is paved with gold—so I just rake it in. Of course, there are plenty of places in the world where the streets are not paved with money, and making money is not the easiest thing in the world to do. It requires a lot of work and plenty of hardship. Nevertheless, I made this joke to show where my real interests are.

An artist who goes to the countryside to paint scenery looks only for good scenery. Someone who goes fishing always remembers the best places to fish. In the same way, an entrepreneur looks for ways to create new business wherever he goes.

I

DREAMING

*Dreams are the power
for changing the world.*

1

History Belongs to Dreamers

I was poor when I was in school, but I was not the only one. Just about everybody was poor at the time: thirty years ago, Korean per capita income was about $70. It is now more than $6,000, so you can imagine how difficult life was for us then. Of course, today there are still poor people, but in the days following the Korean War, dire poverty was widespread.

We lived in the Changchung-dong section of Seoul then, and I had to walk two hours to Yonsei University, which was more than six miles away. I did not have a single coin in my pocket, but I had dreams. I still cannot forget the feeling that would come over me when I stepped out of the library late at night, or when I looked up at the sky on the long trudge home. It seemed like the world was mine, that I could just wrap the universe up in my arms. Nothing seemed impossible to me. The vitality of youth was in me, and it filled my heart with dreams. There was nothing that could stop me.

Of all the things that youth brings with it, dreams are the most important. People with dreams know no poverty, for a person is as rich as his or her dreams. Youth is the time of life when, even if you do not own a thing, you have nothing to envy if you have dreams.

History belongs to dreamers.

Dreams are the power for changing the world. I will bet that all the people who are shaping world history today had big dreams when they were young. The United States, with a history of just over two hundred years, is shaping world history today. And as we know, it was the great dreams of the early settlers with their pioneering spirit that provided the power for such growth.

But nowadays I often hear that young people no longer have dreams about the future. Or that the dreams they do have are fixed only on the present. If that is true, then nothing could be sadder for the individuals, and even more so for the nation.

Dreams often make a person. They control his personality, his work, even his destiny. Dreams are like the rudder of a ship setting sail. The rudder may be small and unseen, but it determines the ship's course. So a life without dreams is like a ship without a rudder. Just as a ship without a rudder becomes nothing but a drifting craft, a person without a dream loses his direction and tosses about until he gets caught in the seaweed.

And a person with the wrong kind of dreams is in as much danger as a person without dreams. A person whose dreams do not go beyond the personal comfort of the present is as pathetic as a person without dreams at all.

I had a dream when five of us started Daewoo Industrial Company. That dream was to contribute to social development through corporate activity. We started with just $10,000 in a small, drab, rented room in the corner of a building, but I had a dream even bigger than the universe itself.

That dream started to come true as the company grew; in just ten years I had the largest building in Korea, today's Daewoo Center. At the time, however, I had my reservations about building the Daewoo Center. I thought it might be better to invest the money into production facilities that would contribute to more immediate economic development. I was also afraid that the company would be criticized for real-estate speculation.

I changed my thinking, however, and started a new dream, a dream to expand the company to the point where we could fill the huge building with Daewoo personnel. At the time such a feat was really unimaginable; yet I realized that dream within five years. Daewoo personnel now number over 100,000—enough to fill three such buildings.

Now I have other dreams. One is to make the finest-quality product in the world during my lifetime. I have already set a number of world records, including the world's largest single dock, at Daewoo Shipbuilding's Okpo Shipyard; the world's largest garment factory, in Pusan; the world's largest-volume garment sales. But there is something that we have not yet achieved, and that is making a product that is the finest of its type in the world.

I treasure this dream, no matter what the product may

turn out to be. It could be anything, as long as it becomes renowned as the finest of its kind in the world—like a Parker pen or a Nikon camera. It does not matter what it is, as long as they say that it was made by Kim Woo-Choong and that it is the best of its kind. That is my dream. But it seems to be a dream that would not be reached easily in the near future. Maybe it will happen only after I pass on the huge Daewoo effort to an outstanding successor.

Another dream, my greatest dream, is to be remembered as a respected entrepreneur. I do not want to be known for being rich or for having made a lot of money.

Traditionally in Korea, businessmen have not been respected; rather, they have been people to look down on or to keep your distance from. There may be a lot of reasons for this, and perhaps the greatest is the deeply rooted Confucian tradition of social rank: the scholar, the farmer, the artisan, and the merchant, in that order, with the merchant at the bottom of the ladder. Another reason can also be found in more recent trends: for some businesspeople, the end—the accumulation of wealth—justifies the means. But I do not see why a businessperson cannot attain the same respect accorded to a professor or an artist.

I want to be remembered as an outstanding professional in my field, and my last dream is to help make a society where entrepreneurs are respected. I will continue to work toward making that dream a reality.

•

*If there is only a 1 percent chance
of success in a project, a true
businessperson sees that 1 percent as
the spark to light a fire.*

•

*In business, you can't just add one
and one and get two. You have to
see one turning into ten, and ten
turning into fifty. That's the way to
count in business.*

•

2

My Philosophy of Life

WHY I'M A BORN OPTIMIST

All through my life, no matter what has happened, I have never discarded my optimism.

Once during my many travels around the world, I was on a plane that had to make an emergency landing; another time a fire broke out in the cabin of the plane during takeoff. Neither time did death even cross my mind—and I guess that shows the *extent* of my optimism. I always think of critical situations as no more than a fleeting moment of danger, and that is the *essence* of my optimism.

I suppose that, in a sense, business is a kind of bloody fight. The bigger the business, the more fights you have and the more you have to pay. If someone in business falls into despair and pessimism in the process, that is the end of his or her development.

One thing that distinguishes me from most other businesspeople is that I have considerable experience in taking over failing firms and turning them around. These firms had been abandoned entirely by their owners, by the banks, and even by the government. Abandonment is pessimism in action. Again and again I have turned chronic failures into profit-making enterprises in practically no time. This has drawn considerable attention from the international press. When asked about it, I always have an answer: "When others start counting the impossibilities, I start counting the possibilities."

At Daewoo, whenever I start any new kind of business or start to trade with a new nation, a number of people worry. When I undertook a refrigerator-plant project in the People's Republic of China, more people were against it than for it. The same thing happened with a joint-venture bank project in Hungary, and when I went off to Moscow to open the Russian market for Daewoo. And resistance was even greater outside the company. Banks and the government were greatly concerned.

But I count differently. I confirm the possibilities, and then quickly work on whatever can turn those possibilities into reality—the type of business, the people, technology, money, machinery, and other requirements.

People who come up with "It may not work" or "What are we going to do if it fails?" do not have the credentials to be businessmen. If there is only a 1 percent chance of success, a true businessperson sees that 1 percent as the spark to light a fire. The business world is not one where you put one and one together to get two, but where you see one turning into ten, and ten turning into fifty. That is how you have to count.

A decade ago we built a tire plant in Sudan. This was the first plant ever built internationally by a Korean firm, and a lot of people had their reservations, because Daewoo had never even dealt in the tire business. But I began by counting the possibilities.

What possibilities? Although Sudan had a market for tires, it had no plant and was losing foreign exchange by importing expensive foreign tires. So I figured the Sudanese would welcome such a project. Sudan is 80 percent desert, and cities are quite far from one another, thereby increasing the demand for ground transportation. Also, I received information from a reliable American source that a huge oil field had been discovered in the southern part of the country.

Such an oil field would greatly bolster economic development, and the demand for cars and trucks would rise proportionately with economic development. For each additional vehicle, there would be demand for at least five tires. And tires wear out much faster in the hot desert than they do in more moderate climates.

That was how I viewed the market. And things have turned out as I calculated. The tire plant is busier than ever now. The plant has undergone a number of expansions, but demand is so great for our tires that now people even pay in advance.

Right from the start, you should be optimistic about whatever you do. But there is one thing that is essential to turn possibilities into reality, and that is dedication.

Also you must have a philosophy of life. People often think of something lofty and difficult when they hear the term "philosophy," but a living philosophy is not so difficult. No matter what you do, dedicate yourself to it. And if you can dedicate yourself to the benefit of society, that is enough.

●

*The spark for creative ideas
comes from hard work
and hard thinking.*

●

3

How to Have Creative Dreams

I f you use your brain, it is developing. Many people say they get more ideas by going to a quiet, relaxing place in the mountains or at the seaside. But actually real ideas come only when the brain cells are moving. The spark for creating ideas comes when you are doing hard work and hard thinking.

And ideas come from input. Your mind must absorb your efforts and experience the way a computer absorbs information you input. It must register everything, and you must keep everything there for future reference. The basic information in your mind can later serve to solve more complex problems.

In my case, working time is when I think best. What's more, creativity increases with hard work. The human brain possesses largely untapped potential—the average person is said to use only 10 percent or so of this gift. Those who work extremely hard can stretch their intuition and insight.

I believe that most people have more potential than they realize or are willing to put to use. So I've tried to make maximum use of my talents in taking on new challenges.

The harder you work by day, the more realistic your dreams are at night. When the brain is full, dreams are fantastic. My experience is that a dream is a wish to accomplish something. When I was young, my father said I should be a businessman. That is the reason that when I was fifteen years old, leading a busy life, I had many dreams at night of being a businessman—dreams that more than came true. If you are in love, you have dreams of being married. If you work hard, your dreams are sometimes solutions to problems.

●

*No one who has poured himself or
herself into work has ever failed.*

●

4

Work Is My Hobby

Every year I spend over two hundred days abroad, and the number of days spent on domestic trips further erodes chances to spend time at home. At times I have forgotten not only my wife's and children's birthdays, but my own as well.

I am busy. And I must admit that I am very happy being busy with so much work, so happy that some people have said that I have gone mad over work. Since I started to work, I have never taken a day off and I do not recall ever having even gone to the beach with my family. Yet I have no regrets.

It is my belief that you are guaranteed success by pouring yourself into your work; no one who has poured himself or herself into work has ever failed.

I suppose that people wonder what on earth a workhorse like me would enjoy in life. They probably cannot figure out why I would become a slave to work rather than mixing business with pleasure and having a little fun.

That type of thinking, however, could come only from people who have never experienced the true joy of work; from people who have never seen the true beauty of a person who pours himself or herself into something completely; from people who have never understood the even greater beauty of a young person completely absorbed in something; from people who have never experienced the utter joy that comes with accomplishment and fulfillment.

I think it is sad that human beings, who are interrelated with everything else in this world, consider work simply as a means to keep their stomachs full. It is even sadder to think that people in the prime of life, who should be filled with great dreams, vitality, and ambition, should feel that work is a nuisance. It is a great insult to the work ethic to think of work, sweat, and effort only in terms of monetary results when you should be thinking of it in terms of accomplishment, fulfillment, personal development, and contribution to society.

Work is something very precious and cannot be evaluated merely in financial terms. It is the same with study. You should study until the point when someone says that you have gone bonkers over studying. Did you ever notice the sparkling eyes of a thoroughly absorbed student?

I tend to get flustered when people ask what my hobbies are because I cannot think of a single "hobby," particularly if a "hobby" is something you do to bide your time. Although occasionally I play a game of Go, I cannot call it a hobby, since that would be an insult to those really good players who do not consider it something you do just to bide your time. I have never played golf, and I have never gone to the theater or to concerts.

If I had to say that I derive a great deal of joy from something, I would have to admit it is work. I have never had to force myself to work, and no one has ever had to force me. So if a hobby is something that brings you joy and satisfaction, then my hobby is work.

If a businessperson handles his or her work spontaneously and takes a hobby-like joy in it, then the business will gradually grow and its facilities will expand. The same thing happens with a student who takes a hobby-like joy in study: the student's marks and standing will improve, and he or she will wind up a prizewinner. If you do not believe me, just give it a try. Trying to be successful without pouring yourself into something is like trying to pluck a star out of the sky; but you cannot fail if you do pour yourself into whatever you are doing, and really enjoy it.

About seven years before I started my own business, I worked for a company run by a distant relative. Although I was part of the family, I was still a regular wage earner; yet I did my work as though I were the owner of the company. I did not wait for orders, and I always took the initiative myself to seek out work to do. I was never late for work and never took a day off. Because of the inexpressible joy I derive from accomplishment, I still work as hard today. For me, the fun of a round of golf or an exciting movie cannot even begin to compare with winning an order at a tug-of-war meeting with prominent international business personalities.

At times I have felt uneasy when approaching a new

person with a new project, the same kind of tension, I suppose, that an athlete must feel when faced with an important test of his or her abilities. But the harder the test and the bigger the project, the greater my concentrated attention and interest. I burst with a rush of fresh energy and vitality after I read the hidden cards and come away successful, when the two of us shake hands in mutual satisfaction over an agreement on a contract that I really wanted.

●

To pioneers, the world is a big place, and there is unlimited work to do.

●

5

It's a Big World Out There

I love to get something going. I am the type of person who cannot sit still very long—a real workaholic. The most difficult thing in the world for me to do is nothing. Some people might call that taking a rest, but not me. Taking a rest for me borders on torture, so I am always on the go. As a result, I have always got my hands into something.

I have no use for getting something started and then forgetting about it, so I like young people who not only get something going, but immerse themselves totally into what they have begun. Because of this intensity of involvement, such people may have a greater chance of failure than, say, people who do not do anything. But, at the same time, they are the kind of people who take a failure or two in stride as part of the experience, and they do not become discouraged. If you have the courage to look at failure this way, then you are on your way to eventual success. Someone who is afraid of failure and afraid to face challenges will never taste success.

It is a big world out there waiting for you, and there is lots to be done. You have to find places that people have never been before, and you have to do things that people have not done before. History has been made by people who have been willing to do those things. These people are the real pioneers.

Of course, there is danger in pioneering, but that is inevitable. Pioneers take paths that have not been paved, and they may even be cursed for it. But danger and criticism do not bother real pioneers; they forge ahead making new paths, and in the end they are praised for what they have done.

History proves that the power and prosperity of nations have been built on the pioneering spirit, and that ruin comes from complacency and evasion of responsibility. Could the United States be as prosperous and powerful as it is if it were not for the pioneering spirit? No one can deny the effect of this spirit on making the United States what it is today.

Although Korea has a long history, it has had little of this pioneering spirit. Throughout history, Koreans have preferred tranquillity over progress and evasion over challenge. We have had a strong tendency to become quickly resigned to situations. Perhaps this is due to our ancient Confucian customs of courtesy and propriety, which in fact have earned the nation such nice names as "the Eastern Land of Etiquette" and "the Land of the Morning Calm." But it is clear that as a result of this historical passivity, we are now far behind world powers in terms of national strength.

When Daewoo was founded, we immediately looked

beyond national borders to the international market at a time when export was generally perceived as a worthless venture. The big companies in those days were all importers and did not give even a thought to export. So we began to pioneer exports, despite everyone's saying that it would not work. We met the challenge and achieved success. The epitome of foolishness is to say something is impossible without even trying.

Daewoo's early spirit of pioneering led us not only to the American and European markets, but to markets in nations with which Korea did not even have diplomatic relations— Sudan, Nigeria, Libya, Angola, Algeria, the People's Republic of China, Vietnam, Hungary, Czechoslovakia, and the Soviet Union. Daewoo's enterprising spirit in opening such markets for Korea eventually led directly to diplomatic relations with Sudan, Libya, Algeria, Nigeria, Hungary, and the Soviet Union.

It is a big world out there waiting, although it may not appear that way to someone who only wants to walk familiar paths and do familiar things. To those people, the world is as narrow as their familiar paths and their work is as limited as familiar habits. To pioneers who are willing to walk new paths and try new things, the world is indeed a big place and there is unlimited work to do. This is how I have lived, and this is how I will go on living—getting new things going and putting everything into them that I can.

●

Don't be fooled by numbers: they inform only of quantity, and this is a major limitation. If you have one hundred pigs and one person, the numbers tell you that it is one hundred to one. Numbers deceive: they can't tell you the strength of the minority.

●

6

The Creative Minority

Today the United States is sometimes described as the falling giant. It's not. True, many people comment that crime, and drugs have been ruining the human character, and many young people are concerned with spending an important part of their lives seeking thrills.

In the midst of all of this, however, there are people who study hard and pour themselves into research for a brighter tomorrow, people who are sweating with efforts to make sure that all of America's great development and progress does not go to waste. I think it is this group that is going to lead America's enormous society.

We should not be fooled by numbers, because they inform us only of quantity, and that is their limitation. For example, if you have a farm with one hundred pigs and one person, numbers by themselves only tell you that it is one hundred to one. So numbers can deceive. They do not tell you the strength of the minority.

Historian Arnold Toynbee referred to those who contribute to civilization as a minority of creative people, a very small minority. But their influence is not determined by their numbers; their influence is determined by their creativity. The creative inspirations of this small minority make it possible for the noncreative majority to participate in the development of history. To do so is not only the right of the creative minority, it is their duty and responsibility; society and history cannot progress without their contributions. These people are obligated to make the noncreative majority change and to make history progress. If they do not, they prompt the end of a society or civilization.

Stifling this minority's creativity also invites the downfall of a society or civilization. When creative capabilities are not used for social advancement, when the creative minority becomes a controlled minority, society is headed toward doom. If leaders fall into hedonism and laziness, then creative inspiration and the spirit to challenge disappear, and doom begins to spread.

You have to become creative and to work creatively for the development, progress, and happiness of society and mankind. You will probably ask how you should go about this, how you should become a creative person, a member of the creative minority. Well, first, let me tell you what you should not do. You should be neither an opportunist nor a mere observer. Nor should you be a defeatist.

What you should have is a broad vision of what you can do for the nation and the people, and furthermore what you can contribute to the history of mankind.

Long, long ago the Hebrews left Egypt and spent forty

years wandering in search of the Promised Land. They were heading for the land of Canaan, which was the land blessed by God. However, the land was already occupied, so the Hebrews sent an expedition of twelve men to check on the overall situation of the Canaanites. When they returned, ten of the twelve men shook their heads, saying that it would be impossible to occupy the land. The inhabitants were much taller than the Hebrews and they had great fortresses. The ten men could see no way that the Hebrews could win a battle.

The other two of the twelve, however, disagreed. They said that the Hebrews had nothing to fear, for it was the land promised to them by God. These men were greatly outnumbered, ten to two. So had the decision to invade been made by majority rule, the Hebrews would have never moved. But based on the arguments of that minority of two, the Hebrews decided to go ahead with their plans, and they succeeded. Majority rule alone does not always shape history. The spirit of challenge by a minority led the Hebrews into the Promised Land.

The creative minority is affirmative. It is composed of people who keep the spark of hope and optimism in the middle of uncertainty and despair. The creative minority believes in the progress of history, and gives added impetus for progress and development to the wheels of history.

●

If you are just holding your own, others are passing you by. Maintaining the status quo is regressing.

●

7

Who Will Wake the
Sleeping Genius?

Perhaps you have heard the story of a frail mother who lifted up a whole automobile to save her son stuck under it. It is an example of our tremendous latent powers. Humans possess fantastic capabilities, but because these capabilities usually remain latent within us we are not always aware of them. The people who discover this potential become successes; the ones who do not just go about living ordinary lives. If we used 20 percent of our true potential, we would all be geniuses, and if we used 30 percent we could be great heroes.

So it is fair to say that anyone who is a genius or a hero has developed his latent capabilities to a greater extent than the average person. Edison often repeated the same experiment two hundred times or more before inventing something. He became a genius by relentlessly developing his latent potential, by waking the sleeping genius within.

You have to develop yourself creatively. The French philosopher Henri Bergson once said that making progress was the very nature of life. All that lives has to develop actively; this is often called the principle of life.

So you have to watch constantly your progress and exert yourself to become brighter, smarter, and better. You must be generous with others, but severe with yourself, and you have to be careful not to fall into the traps of excuses and rationalizations. If you think of yourself as a wimp, then others will think of you that way as well.

I always regret that I did not study more in college. I had plans to study abroad, but circumstances at the time did not allow me, so perhaps that is why I still feel that I have missed something. And I feel it all the more when I see my own inadequacies as I travel around the world meeting all kinds of people. It becomes a problem, for example, if you do not know much about the history and customs of a nation when you have to meet a foreigner on business.

When you travel, you never know what kind of religious beliefs or interests the person you are meeting might have, so you have to be prepared for every possible situation. Otherwise, things may not go so smoothly. For example, do you know anything about Islam and Hinduism, or about the history of Sudan and Algeria?

I sometimes take college professors with me on my trips so that they can brief me concerning the nation I am visiting. These briefings broaden my knowledge of the history, social conditions, recent events, and other facets of these nations. Of course, it is like sightseeing from a passing train, but it does invigorate me and give me new strength as well as additional knowledge.

Maintaining the status quo is the same as regressing; while you are holding your own, others are passing you by. It is no exaggeration to say that it is all over for someone who lives that way, because such a person has no expectations for further development. Only those people who continually develop themselves and study earnestly will make progress.

Be harsh on yourself. Do not ever think that you have made it; do not ever be satisfied with what you have done. Drive yourself for the rest of your life. If you do not move, you become paralyzed. Develop your potential to the fullest, for you, too, can wake the sleeping genius at will.

•

*Share your knowledge. Intellectual
selfishness is as bad as material
selfishness.*

•

8

What Is True Happiness?

K nowledge has always been greatly valued, and I grew up at a time when such phrases as "Don't give away your knowledge" and "You have to know something to become something" were popular. Those words were a living lesson taught to me by my grandfather and father, who knew through their own experiences the value of learning and knowledge. The world is structured to accommodate those who study hard, and those old sayings are just as valid today as they were decades ago.

I do have reservations, however, about the saying "Don't give away your knowledge," which reflects a certain coldness and selfishness. I would prefer "Share your knowledge," for it is the responsibility of the learned to give others a chance to learn. And this generosity should not be limited to learning alone: we should share everything with our fellow man. We should share our knowledge and we should share our money, for intellectual selfishness and material selfishness are equally bad. It is important to live for others. As soon as you start living for others, the world becomes brighter and warmer and happier. Life becomes worth living.

I had my first taste of real happiness selling papers in Taegu when we were refugees during the Korean War. In those days, because of the war, people were so destitute that it was easier to die than to live. We were constantly hungry, and yet it was one of those ironies of life that hunger gave us the courage to live.

With my father kidnapped and taken north and my older brothers in the army, I was, at age fourteen, responsible for feeding the family. I had to sell at least a hundred newspapers in the market a day to cover basic expenses; my mother and younger brothers waited late into the night for me to come home so that we could all eat together. I was always very grateful to them for that. I really felt great when the four of us ate together. I was so happy, and we really enjoyed those meals.

But we could not always eat as a family. The Pangchon market in Taegu where I sold the papers was largely makeshift shacks along the river, and often the shops would close during inclement weather. I had to sell my one hundred papers if we were to eat, so bad weather meant trouble. On some days I had only a few extra coins to give the family for the day's meals on my way out in the morning.

When I came home on those nights, my mother and brothers would be sleeping, and I quickly came to realize why they were sleeping: there was only one bowl of rice, and they were saving it for me. My mother would get up to feed me and say, "We've already eaten. You must be hungry, so hurry up and eat."

I thought I would cry when I looked at my brothers, whom my mother had put to bed hungry because there was only one bowl of rice. But I hid my tears as well as my mother hid hers. I told her that I had had a bowl of noodles on the way home, and that she and the other kids should eat. We were obviously lying to each other and we both knew it, but how could we otherwise express our feelings?

We were materially poor, but we were rich at heart. We had very little, but gave to one another what we could. Someone who has everything in the world but does not know how to give is not rich. The really rich people are the people who give a lot, people who give what they can, people who know how to give no matter how little or how much they have.

What is true happiness? I cannot really say that I know for sure, but I do know that it does not have very much to do with possessions, power, or fame. I can say that I remember being happiest at a time when we had the least materially.

Since that time, I have tried to practice a philosophy based on living for others, but I have come to learn how very difficult that is. Yet I have decided to try even harder to live that way.

II

MANAGING

●

Business is more than making money; losing less money is sometimes important too.

●

9

Management by Objective Is Not Enough

MAKING DECISIONS ON THE SPOT

Some of my most valuable management techniques are not taught even at American business schools. They train students in "management by objective" through four major steps: planning, organizing, leading, and controlling. I would add two more vital steps. A top executive should create and follow up. So there are six steps, not four. Moreover, a big organization must have flexibility to adapt to changing situations and must make quick decisions. That's why I travel so much. Most of the countries I go to have big uncertainties and changes, so I like to make decisions on the spot, not from a report or analysis by others. And changes come much faster in business than they used to, thus requiring more concentration on innovation in economics, in politics, and in other areas.

In developing countries, where I do a lot of business, regulations often change. Sometimes they have money, sometimes they do not. Exchange rates fluctuate widely. Many risks are greater than normal. If you delay a decision, it costs you. No armchair analyst can run this kind of business. You must know the total situation. In each country you need to meet bankers, friends, government officers, and others to obtain total information—the full picture at that moment.

Executives find it very hard to make decisions sometimes when faced with many uncertainties. But business is more than making money; losing less money is sometimes important, too. A big company moves like a continuously rolling snowball. But when you're in a losing period, the healthy thing is managing to cut the losses. So I travel to get immediate, up-to-date information and make decisions on the spot.

For example, when we first entered the Vietnamese market, I sent a survey team to study the possibilities for business in Vietnam. That gave me information. Then I went to see for myself, to get confirmation of the information. During discussions, I spotted business opportunities—like establishing a joint venture for making textiles. I suggested that rather than bringing in new equipment, we could use some of the idle spindles in Korea. They were not being used because of a lack of personnel and because higher wages were moving Korea to automate. I knew there were 500,000 Korean spindles sitting idle. I could buy them for 20 percent of their cost. I went to see the Vietnamese factories and studied their salaries, which showed me this was feasible. They had twenty-to-thirty-year-old equipment, while our idle spindles were only ten years old. Vietnam was short of foreign exchange, but had a good work force. Seeing the Vietnamese factories, I immediately made a decision to bring in the old Korean machines. Instead of $100 million investment for our venture, $20 million was now enough. The building already existed, along with ample electricity, water, and workers.

Changing the equipment would take time, so I decided to ask our Vietnamese partner to send at least 30 percent of its engineers and technicians to Korea, where we could put them to work in a factory and train them for six months. Then they could go home and produce better. The factory in Vietnam would pay for the machinery by producing goods that we would buy. I made this decision on the spot and signed a contract.

If a European textile company went there, I don't think it could make decisions on the spot. Americans would want to study everything for a while. But I got all the information, went there, and made a decision.

Business in Third World countries is never just a single transaction. We needed local money to operate that joint-venture factory in Vietnam. Rather than bringing in cash, I brought in merchandise, which could be sold in the market for a profit because Vietnam is short of everything.

Within one business we can have many other businesses. If we have too much local currency, we buy products to export and earn foreign exchange that way. This is the best thing to do when there's inflation in a country. If you go to a country— and evaluate all the information—you can create other business "on the spot."

Many people might look at a country without money and figure that it's hopeless. They don't really see all the possibilities for creating business. I went into a joint venture in Burma to make television sets and radios, but many people couldn't see how we could get foreign exchange to import the components. Domestic demand for consumer electronic products is strong in Burma. I earn a lot of local money, so we immediately decided to build a hotel. The hotel will generate foreign exchange. I can also buy rice and export it to earn foreign exchange to pay for electronic components. Others often see only the risk and do nothing, but I look for the possibilities.

In Eastern Europe, every country has debt, and many businessmen say that it is ridiculous to try to do business there. I go there—and see things differently. In Yugoslavia, for example, we are developing other opportunities by purchasing wheat. The local interest rate for deposits there is 20 percent monthly, so I paid in advance for two months and got a large discount on the wheat. I can sell that wheat in the Middle East at the international price and earn a profit. Other wheat shipments will be paid for by bartering our autos and electronic goods, on which we make a profit, too.

I handle these kinds of special transactions myself, because they depend on knowing the situation around the world and being able to make quick decisions. The Daewoo staff, of course, helps me and does the follow-up work.

You have to be sharply attuned to markets in each country to do this kind of business. Vietnam, for example, has to buy a lot of fertilizer and normally gets it from countries like Indonesia. The supplier sells it and the deal is finished. Anybody could do that business. But I don't do that. Instead I go to the Russians and tell them I want fertilizer, not for cash, but for goods they need. I give them textile products in barter. A normal person goes to buy and sell for 50 percent profit and is finished. This is no good. If we have a chance, we must utilize our buying power and selling power at 100 percent.

I'm training people in my office to do this kind of business, but the problem is that none of them has all the information. I have more information—and unlimited ideas for using it. When I hear things during my travels, I can cook up these transactions. You cannot get this kind of information through telex messages or reading, but only through conversation, knowing people, and understanding business conditions that are constantly changing.

●

No matter what the issue, it is up to the executive to make the final decision.

●

10

A Lesson in Making Decisions

I had an experience in Belgium that taught me a great lesson.

My connections with Antwerp began in 1984, when I got an unexpected offer to take over a company's oil refinery in the city. I first had the director of the Daewoo London branch investigate the company through London financial markets. I also sent a manager who was an expert on the international oil market to investigate the company in Antwerp.

From the reports of our people, I learned that the company had had considerable labor disputes and was running in the red. The president of the company had already made offers to renowned Japanese, German, and American companies to take it over; all had refused. I concluded that the company was not in very good financial shape.

I asked for the opinion of our manager who went to inspect the company. He said that although the facilities were quite old, the plant, with a little renovation, would be operable. He found that the workers felt that the company president had little interest in the plant and that the rest of the managerial staff had a greater interest in closing down than in trying to save the company.

So the final decision rested with me. And I made it based upon the results of an accurate survey of two facets of operations.

First, the facilities were old, but still capable of producing 65,000 barrels of oil a day. The price of $1.5 million for the entire plant was much lower than the cost of building a new facility.

The second consideration was the work force. I diagnosed its low morale as a direct result of the president's indifference and the staff's negligence. I decided that the project was possible if we dispatched superior managerial power to bring about a complete change in attitude. I felt that the work force, tired of an old, indifferent administration with which it had struggled for years, would have a change of heart with a fresh new administration.

A third problem was oil, and this is where I had the greatest confidence. I already had a promise from the government of Libya for a certain volume of crude oil. When Libya started having foreign exchange problems, we had worked out a barter agreement for crude in exchange for a huge apartment construction project. Owning a refinery could be a wise investment for us, since there is greater profit in refined oil than in crude. Of course, there was always the chance that the consumer market for gasoline, kerosene, and other refined oil would not be so great. If there was not great demand, we could first sell some crude and then sell refined oil when the market recovered.

Based on these considerations, I gave directives to go ahead with the takeover immediately. The following year, once the takeover was finalized, we selected and dispatched a crack team of administrators to Antwerp. We changed the name to Universal, to be consistent with Daewoo, which means "great universe." Everything was done to create an entirely new atmosphere at the company.

In less than a year, the results of our efforts were not only obvious but dramatic. The work force had new strength and energy to cooperate with management. And I think they learned a thing or two from the example set by Daewoo personnel. Within a year, the company had turned around and made a profit. After that, sales went so well that we got an offer from the former president to buy back the company at five times the price we had paid for it. As a result of this success, I developed something of an international reputation as a turnaround expert.

But the reason I treasure the Antwerp project is not the fame I got from it or the profit. I treasure it because of the lesson it provided me in the importance of decision-making.

Renowned firms in the United States, Japan, Germany, and England were all approached with the proposal, and they investigated the possibilities. But they all turned it down based on superficialities. Perhaps they quickly dropped consideration after surveying the financial status of the company. In any case, they made rather awkward assessments, and thereby lost the chance to make quite a bit of money.

I had a similar experience in Korea with the Korea Machinery Company. The company was first formed during the Japanese occupation to build Japanese submarines. When we took over the company, it had not made a profit in its forty-odd years of existence and was in very bad shape.

Before coming to us, the government had approached two other large Korean conglomerates. Both conducted a number of extensive surveys. Based on the results of the surveys and future prospects of the company, they both turned the offer down. Then the offer came to me, and I conducted the exact same surveys; and based on the same results, I decided to take over the company. We changed the name to Daewoo Heavy Industries Limited, and it is now a leader in the Korean machinery industry.

When doing business, you run into a lot of decision-making situations. Sometimes these decisions are minor, and sometimes they can affect the entire fortune of a company. But no matter what the issue, it is up to the executive to make the final decision. Over the years, I have worked with innumerable colleagues, but my loneliest moments are when I have to make a decision.

My colleagues and staff, of course, provide me with all kinds of information and help. But because of the responsibilities involved, they cannot make the final decision for me. Just as I cannot make others responsible for myself, I cannot make them responsible for my decisions.

Decision-making is important not only in business—it is important throughout life. Life is a series of decisions, and one wrong decision can ruin a life. I sometimes wonder whether we are living just to be able to have the chance to make the one right decision that will lead to success.

●

A little help can be invaluable.

●

11

The Toughest Sale I Ever Made

The first time that I faced difficulty making a sale was when I came to Chicago in the early 1970s and approached Sears to buy our shirts. We were already supplying American importers, but I wanted to go directly to the big department stores. It's not easy for a small company to go knocking on doors to make sales, but that's what I did. And it was one of the most exciting periods of my life.

In those days nobody knew Daewoo. Our people told me that you needed an appointment to see buyers at a department store like Sears. But if a buyer's secretary announced that Daewoo was calling for an appointment, the buyer would certainly ask: "Who's Daewoo?" Without knowing our company, he or she would never give us a chance. So I decided to go visit

Sears, bringing along my sample cases. Once there, I knew we would have a better chance of meeting a buyer.

The first day that I went to Sears, they didn't say no, but told us to wait. The buyer had no time, even though I waited for two hours. So the next day I returned and talked with the receptionist. It was hard to meet even a secretary. I kept going back for several days until a buyer finally agreed to see me. I never got discouraged. If I had to come back ten times, that would not bother me—as long as I got to see the buyer. I had confidence. Why not? Sears needed good vendors, and we could meet their requirements.

Finally, I got to see Jim Weiss, the senior buyer of men's shirts at Sears. Then everything was easy. During our first meeting, Mr. Weiss seemed to have confidence in me. I explained everything very logically and sincerely, which maybe surprised him. I offered to install any facility needed to meet Sears's requirements, promised to keep delivery dates, and set good prices. There was room to cut our price and still make a profit, because I would not be selling through importers. Sears gave me a small test order, and then our business gradually increased to a peak of some $200 million a year. Even now we still supply shirts to Sears.

After we got our first big orders, I installed a test lab exactly like the one at Sears. It was a big investment for us in those days, but I didn't care, because we needed to produce quality goods. We gave Sears all the test reports. Mr. Weiss and other buyers visited our factory in Korea, and they were happy to see that lab. We followed their system of quality control and inspection. Soon the shirt buyers at Sears were pro-Kim and introduced me to buyers of other products. We developed more than a hundred items for Sears—leather goods, handbags, shoes, baseball gloves. As a small company, we took great pride in supplying one of the biggest stores in the United States.

If we had failed to open the door at Sears, then maybe I would not have gained the confidence to export other products, such as cars, to the United States. Once we sold to Sears, of course, then it was easy to supply other big American retailers. When you're a young company, a little help is invaluable. Sears helped me a lot because I worked hard for it. Our relationship became like that of a family.

Now I do everything possible to provide opportunities for Sears. Recently, Korea opened its market to foreign life insurance companies, and I recommended Sears to our government: Daewoo and Allstate (a Sears company) have a joint venture for insurance. I'd like to bring Sears stores and credit cards into Korea, too.

•

More meetings can mean more confusion, not less.

•

Make easy decisions first; it gets them out of the way.

•

12

How to Avoid Long Business Meetings,

OR HOW TO ABSORB INFORMATION QUICKLY

American executives complain that they spend a large part of the working day at company meetings. In the United States, decisions are made by groups of managers, not by a top executive. That is why American executives have so many meetings. Keeping everybody happy doesn't bring good results. Sometimes too many meetings just spreads confusion. There are many changes in business conditions, so decisions cannot be made theoretically. You must have the feel, the smell, of each situation, plus experience, to get the right information and make the right decisions.

Meetings are justified for getting information. But I don't think you need that much detail. Whenever I get a three-page report, I feel that half a page would be enough. In written reports managers often go on for two or three pages when one sentence would be enough. The top executive needs only the key things to make a decision.

I don't see many documents. I hear them. That saves me time and keeps me from being too tired. Instead of reading reports, I give them to an assistant, who tells me the main points and what questions are raised. Mostly, executives come to me without paper and make a report. I hear it, and then make a decision. To save time, I tell them to bring written reports to my office, so I can ask questions and ask for an opinion. If it's a very important matter, I'll read the document right there. I ask the executive for his or her decision. If it's right, I will say, "Go ahead." I want my executives to take responsibility, rather than asking me to decide everything. About half the things executives bring to me they could decide themselves. Frequently, I ask them why they didn't just do that. Then they don't come to me as often.

When people come to see me, I take the easy things first, the ones we can do in five to ten minutes. Serious matters that take time we talk about on Sunday or in the late evening.

Every Monday morning at 8:00 we have a meeting of the top fifteen executives, and I inform them about what I've been doing abroad and so forth. Sometimes that meeting, which is a good way to share information, can last until lunchtime. If it takes longer, we meet again—on Sunday, on Saturday afternoon, or in the evening.

●

Rice has to be in a bowl to be eaten. Once it touches the floor it becomes inedible.

●

13

No One Eats Off the Floor

THE SECRET OF GOOD JOB PLACEMENT

Everyone and everything has a place in life.

There is order and peace only when everything is where it belongs. When things are not right, there is chaos and confusion. Think of it: what would it be like if your eyes were where your nose is, your ears at your mouth and your mouth at your eyes? Your eyes are there because they should be, and the same goes for your nose and your mouth. That is normal, and the organs are harmonized. There is peace, harmony, and order when things are where they belong.

It is very important that we have food, for we have to eat.

But, for example, rice has to be in a bowl to be eaten. No one would eat rice off the floor, because once it touches the floor it becomes inedible. If rice is eaten from a bowl it becomes a source of human energy, but if it falls to the floor it gets tossed out with the rest of the garbage.

So everything should be in its place; when it is not, there is trouble. Problems arise when you are not doing what you are supposed to be doing. Students should be students, parents should be parents, workers should be workers, and entrepreneurs should be entrepreneurs; social problems arise when they are not.

We all have to be doing what we should be doing if we want and expect rapid social development and stability. Workers should not be leaving the workplace and nonworkers should not be taking their place. The same principle is true for students and soldiers and parents.

Our personnel policy is based on putting the right person in the right place, because that is essential to making the company run smoothly. People are placed according to their abilities and capabilities, so it is unusual for us to give double promotions. But because of differences in capabilities, some people rise faster than others on the corporate ladder.

Putting the right person in the right place is the most important task of the personnel department. Up until just a few years ago I did the selection of all managers myself. Now that the company presidents know my policy, they do it directly.

There was a popular song in Korea that went, "Turning, turning, the chair is turning, and it belongs to whoever sits in it. . . ." That, however, is not the case. Each chair has its proper occupant, and he or she is the one who should sit in it and do the work that goes with it. This is what is proper. There is trouble when someone who does not belong there takes the seat and either does not do the work or does not do it properly. Everybody has an appropriate seat, so to speak, and when people are where they belong, society functions well, things are quiet, and everything goes smoothly.

●

When mistakes are made, the top executive has to take responsibility.

●

14

Why I Promote Executives from Within the Company

American companies frequently hire a chief executive from another corporation, but I don't believe that is effective. Everything in business is done through knowing people. And promoting executives from within your company means they will know more about your business.

Anyone who works hard can be a capable manager, but you have to find out who is the best person for a particular job within the company. When you expand, you need someone to drive forward aggressively. After expansion, you need another kind of manager to tighten up and consolidate. Then when business is dull, you need a driving kind of manager again.

Without knowing the character of managers, it's very hard to judge them. How can a senior executive brought in from outside the company know the managers and have loyalty from them?

Work is done by getting your executives to work hard. Whenever mistakes are made, the top executive has to take responsibility. That way the other managers have more confidence in the boss, and he or she can choose the right person for each job.

•

*Big opportunities should follow
rigorous duties.*

•

15

How to Find the World's Best Assistant,

E very three years I select a young man right out of university to serve as my personal assistant, an extremely tough job. I pick him from among five candidates after many intensive interviews. After all, this person is being given a big opportunity. I also give him very rigorous duties. My personal assistant reports to my home early every morning to brief me on appointments and telephone messages, and he finishes late that night by riding home with me. He's with me more than my wife. Whenever I travel—and I'm on the go more than two hundred days a year—the personal assistant always has to accompany me. I allow no exceptions to this. He does everything from carrying the luggage to taking notes on important meetings for follow-up action. My assistant, of course, never gets a vacation for three years, because I don't go on vacation. But he learns a great deal about our group—especially its work ethic—by watching and studying what I do.

This job of personal assistant is more for training young people than for doing the necessary work. After three rugged years, I give each assistant a choice of going abroad for gradu-ate study at the company's expense or going directly into a manager's job. They get promoted quicker than others because they have worked harder and longer. One recent assistant, for instance, already had a Ph.D. in engineering from MIT, and now he's in our auto company. Several other of my former personal assistants are executive vice presidents of Daewoo companies. Working with me is an ideal training program.

•

One mistake is a great teacher; two mistakes is one too many.

•

16

What to Do with an Employee Who Gambles Away the Company's Money

I always give someone who makes a mistake another chance. That person is greater because he or she has gained experience. One of my employees based overseas went to a casino and lost $10,000 of the company's money—which would certainly get him fired by a normal manager. I didn't fire him, but paid the money back to the company myself and gave him a second chance. If it happened again, then I would have to let him go. But I had a good reason for keeping him: if he has the confidence to beat a casino dealer, then I want him to use it to create business. His kind of brain can generate bigger things for the company. That man, in fact, has gone on to do very well. I don't want to lose people like that because of a momentary lapse.

There is a very young senior executive at Daewoo, a man whose father once told me he was a big headache. He's from a very good family, but while studying in the United States he was betting on horse races and many other things. I hired him as my personal assistant, a very important job in the company. He changed his ways, followed my spirit, and was promoted like a skyrocket. Whenever I give him a job, he completes it. Sometimes he's better than I am. Now he's a very young president of a Daewoo subsidiary. You can develop great talent by giving people a chance to learn from their mistakes.

•

You don't have to read a report for
it to be effective.

•

17

How to Energize Lazy Executives

ometimes when I notice that a president of one of my group's twenty-two companies is not working very hard, I will ask him to write a two-hundred-page detailed report on his operations every three months. Then I just file his reports. The executive thinks I have read them. But writing those reports is the important thing, because he has to check closely on all aspects of his company, and it keeps him very busy. Finding out everything that's going on is good—for him. Sometimes I read a little of the reports, of course, so I can ask a few questions. This is a good cure for lazy managers.

•

*Most innovations are based on
simple ideas.*

•

18

The Importance of Innovation—and How to Do It

Once I was invited to speak at a managers' training seminar at a daily newspaper in Seoul. I was asked to give a one-hour speech on the subject "Corporate Management and My Managerial Philosophy." Rarely was a businessperson invited to speak before a newspaper group, and I would have to be careful when speaking to such an audience. Out of courtesy if nothing else, however, I found it difficult to turn down the invitation.

So I talked for an hour on my thoughts concerning corporate management, and what I said was quite compatible with the trends for managerial reform at the time. Toward the end, one manager abruptly asked, "If you were managing a newspaper, what would you do to innovate?"

I had always been an outsider to the newspaper business, and it was difficult enough going to the seminar to make the speech. To be hit with such an unexpected question completely flustered me.

But something came to mind, and that was *Kobawu,* a highly popular comic strip on contemporary society, a strip I greatly enjoyed. I had observed that most people first read the leading story on the front page and, if there is not anything else of particular interest, they quickly turn to the social pages at the back of the paper. And there the first thing to attract attention is this comic strip in the upper corner of the inside back page.

Advertisers always want the places that catch the reader's eye. Consequently, prices for such spots correspond to their popularity. Every time I read the comic strip, I thought like a businessperson: "Since people have such reading habits, placing an ad in the comic strip section would naturally draw a lot of attention. It would really work if the comic ran for five days, and then you placed an ad on the sixth day in the same slot. If that could not be done, then lengthening the comic strip from four blocks to five, and putting an ad in the middle of the strip would work well." Such a precious spot on the *Kobawu* comic strip would, no doubt, be the envy of every businessperson. So I said this in response to the manager's question.

Not too long after that, I noticed the *Kobawu* comic strip had been lengthened to five blocks—with an advertisement in the fifth one.

Innovation is essential to life, and it is not as hard as you might think. That is something I stress wherever I go. The problem is not the innovation itself, but whether or not you want to innovate. If you look carefully at really worthwhile inventions, most of them are actually based on quite simple ideas, which often bring about great results. Innovation plays a highly important role in corporate management as well.

Innovation has played a prominent role in the history of mankind. It begins with the determination of a creative person to break with contemporary reality by making something new. I have always emphasized the importance of being creative, because creative people make history and keep the world moving.

Developing creativity begins with asking questions about the present situation: "Have I tried my best?" "Is the current situation ideal?" "Can we make a better product?" "Isn't there a better method?" Such probing stimulates your latent creativity; the more you probe, the greater your results will be.

When I first went to work after college, I was responsible for dealing with a bank on behalf of a new company, Hansung Industrial. It was rather easy work: all I had to do was submit company documents to the bank, which either accepted them for higher approval or rejected them. If the papers were rejected, the company would make the necessary changes and I simply resubmitted them.

The person who held this position before I joined the company had a tough time with the job, however. He spent much of the day going back and forth between the company and the bank. Drawing up the documents took quite a bit of time, and if they were rejected, he lost even more time. So shortly after I took the job, I carefully watched all processes to discover problems. I became a troubleshooter.

I decided that the first step was to establish a good relationship with the women at the bank who accepted the documents, because it was up to them to decide whether or not the papers went on to get higher approval. If, by chance, there was a minor mistake, the women could correct it and send the papers on. But there was also the problem of competition: numerous companies were submitting similar documents, and the lower your paper in the pile, the longer your company had to wait for approval.

At the time, we had a storeroom filled with imported Italian blouse fabric that was not selling—and the person responsible for it was not taking care of the situation. So I put the two together: the fabric was just sitting there, and the women at the bank might like the material. I figured that by selling the material to them cheaply, I would actually be making a profit for the company in more ways than one. Each day the fabric sat in the storehouse, the company was losing not only potential profit, but also potential interest on the profit as well.

The fabric made a hit with the women at the bank, and they even got their friends to buy it. They liked the new fabric as well as the price—and at the same time we were clearing out the company warehouse. From then on, the papers I brought to the bank got top priority.

The second problem was that I was still stuck with a lot of paperwork that I thought could be reduced by half. This also was easier to solve than I thought. The types of documents were limited, and only a few figures would vary with each document. All the other things were fixed: the company's name, the applicant's seal, the addressee, and so forth. So whenever I had any spare time, I prepared as many documents as possible ahead of time. All the company had to do was fill in the figures and dates.

Things had improved, but I was still going to the bank several times a day. By probing, I discovered that only two dispatches a day were necessary, one in the morning and one in the afternoon. The person who had preceded me on the job had never taken the time to notice that documents submitted to the bank in the morning were approved in the late afternoon, and those submitted in the afternoon were approved the next morning. Unaware of this, he had been spending the whole day running back and forth to the bank with a different document each time. He was merely doing what he had been taught by his predecessor or superior, and he had never thought of innovating to save time, money, and even his own shoe leather. I decided to change our work pattern to fit the bank's schedule.

Only a month after I had the job, I was promoted and praised as some kind of genius. At the time, a promotion was considered a real feat for a new employee. But the success of my debut was due only to my ability to perceive problems and to improve the existing situation. As the years passed, I continued to sharpen my problem-solving abilities and to improve my capabilities at innovating. I can confidently say that the ability to make Daewoo grow the way it did was due to managerial innovation in both large and small ways.

•

*Always work and live with the
mentality of an owner.*

•

19

Think As If You Own the Company

Those of you who have grown up in the city probably don't know about a certain type of weed that grows alongside rice. Country folk have to weed constantly for the rice to grow properly.

The farmer will tell the farmhand to go out and weed the paddies, and the farmhand will go out and work all day. But the next day the farmer will still find weeds. He can send the farmhand time and again, but still there will be weeds until the farmer goes out and pulls them out himself.

Why? Because the farmer, as owner of the paddies, takes great interest in his land. But the farmhand does not have such concern because it is not his land.

Because the farmer is an owner, he actively looks for things to do in caring for his land. He does not ask himself why he should have to do things when other people are not doing them. He knows what he has to do without anyone telling him. The farmhand, however, does not look for work to do, and asks why he has to do something when others do not have to do it. If he is not told what to do, he does nothing. He just takes it easy.

You see the difference in the mentalities of a farm owner and a farmhand. If we look closely at the decline of socialist economies today, we can see that it has a lot to do with the mentalities I am talking about: almost everyone is a farmhand.

If you look around, you will notice people who not only do what they have to, but also do work for others without having to be told. You will also notice, on the other hand, people who do not do their own work unless told to, let alone do work for others. Again, the difference can be found in the ownership mentality and the farmhand mentality.

You should always work and live with the mentality of an owner. Someone with such a mentality is not bothered by circumstances. He or she is creative, challenges things, and overflows with determination. Employees who work with this ownership mentality make companies successful. People who have the farmhand mentality find it sufficient to earn a month's pay by doing only what they are told by superiors. And maybe they work hard at it. But the company will never be successful.

About a decade ago, on a sultry summer day, shortly after we first began international construction projects, I saw a long line of people standing outside the company offices as I stepped out on business. It did not look like a particularly friendly event, and on my way back to the company I noticed that most of the people were women, some of whom even had children on their backs. Everyone was sweating in the summer heat. I asked what was going on, and was told that they were families of employees working overseas.

All of those family members were standing out in the blazing sun, but the officials who were supposed to be dealing with them were sitting cool and comfortable in an air-conditioned office. Feeling sorry for the women and children out there in the sun, since they, too, were members of the Daewoo family, I took the office workers to task, and I let the person in charge of the office have a piece of my mind. I asked the office manager if he could go out and stand in the sun for even five minutes.

His excuse was that the office was too small to accommodate all the people outside. I found that unacceptable. Responsibility has no room for excuses. If the manager thought of the company as his own and thought of the people outside as being in effect members of the company, he would have been able to figure out something. There was no excuse whatsoever for leaving so many people out in the hot blazing sun for so long.

One of the worst things in the world is to stand on the sidelines. If you become filled with excuses and lack a sense of ownership, then you easily fall into mediocrity and the indifference of a mere observer, a mere bystander. Unfortunately, some people refer to this as "the age of the bystander."

•

A "good enough" finish mocks all the sweat and effort that go into the making of a product.

•

20

Beware of the Suitability Syndrome

WHY JUST GETTING BY NEVER WORKS

I still have a recurring dream, one in which I fail to graduate from college. In fact, I almost did not graduate, which I suppose explains why I keep having this dream. During my last semester in college, I did part-time work for a government agency instead of going to classes. In those days in Korea, seniors took graduation for granted and did just about everything except attend classes.

Of course, seniors, myself included, were busy trying to find jobs, but this "We've made it!" type of mentality was a larger factor in absenteeism from classes, an expected form of behavior for all seniors at the time.

One of my final courses was with Professor Whang Il-Chong, who now teaches at Hanyang University in Seoul. He had recently returned from studying in the United States, and was highly impressed with the rational educational atmosphere there.

I was unaware that Professor Whang took attendance every day and refused to grade anyone who was absent a certain number of times. I found out too late and was in a dilemma: if I did not get a grade from him, I would not graduate.

So I went to see Professor Whang and pleaded with him to let me graduate. He was unmoved. I think he misunderstood me as being a completely irresponsible student, and I had a hard time convincing him otherwise. At the time, I was president of the Business Students Friendship Association, and I even went as far as to get members of the association to visit him at his home and plead my case.

At last, Professor Whang gave in on the condition that I write and submit a special report, which I did, and I did graduate. But it was a good lesson to me in overcoming the "suitability syndrome." A senior should be as diligent as a freshman, perhaps even more so; but I had been thinking only in terms of *passing* my time *suitably* until graduation. I felt that what I had already learned in school was good enough. The lesson I learned through the experience made such an impression that I still dream about it!

Consequently, since starting my own business I have not tolerated any of this "good enough" syndrome among workers. It offers nothing for either the individual or society at large.

* * *

Over the years, I have sold countless products internationally and I have encountered one recurring, troublesome problem: the finished product. Korean products have been recognized for their design, quality, and prices, but the finishing of the product has always been a thorn in my side and an excuse for buyers to cut the price even further. It means not only a loss on the price of the product, but loss of face to me as a Korean.

This has always distressed me, because a "good enough" finish mocks all the sweat and effort that went into the making of the product. And this has resulted in great loss to the nation.

We can easily find instances of this suitability syndrome. When I first started Daewoo in 1967, virtually all export products were shipped. The shipping industry was not very developed, and consequently there was great competition to get a shipment loaded and sent. So most of the export companies had representatives at the port in Pusan.

Things were pretty frantic when it came to meeting foreign delivery deadlines. Production plants buzzed around the clock. After the products reached the customs clearance warehouses in Pusan, company representatives had to wait their turn to get a ship. If we failed to secure a ship in time, we would have to wait at least a week for another one, and all the strenuous production effort would have gone for naught. The entire fortune of smaller companies rested on securing a ship in time, so the pressure on company representatives at the docks was tremendous.

Naturally, the competition among these representatives was fierce. Representatives who were not completely alert could easily be outdone by their competitors. There were even instances where one company's goods were loaded onto a ship, but after the representative left satisfied, the goods were unloaded and replaced by goods from another company.

It was interesting to observe that there were three types of company representatives at the port. The first type left after confirming arrival of their company's goods at the dock. The second type would confirm arrival at the dock and stay until the goods were loaded. But the third type of representative stayed to confirm the ship's departure.

Representatives of the first type often lost out, and those of the second type lost once or twice out of ten chances. But representatives of the third type were always successful. The first two types of representative were doing what they thought was good enough at the time, but it often ended in failure for their companies.

I ordered the representatives of our company to stay on the dock until the ship was actually beyond the horizon. That was finishing the product, so to speak. As a result, we did not lose a single shipment at the dock, and our deliveries were always on time. This was highly essential in establishing a reputation for reliability with international clients. The word got around that Daewoo could be trusted to deliver.

No matter what I do, I like to do it thoroughly. That is the key to success. And I have instilled this principle of doing things thoroughly in our employees. This is a principle that people should apply to everything, not just products. Doing your very best until the very end is not only important, it is essential. This has become a tradition at Daewoo and the very essence of Daewoo corporate culture.

●

When faced with a new and complicated market, here is a foolproof way to narrow it: identify the richest sector, the sector with the most land, and the sector with the most people. Concentrate all your efforts on those three. The rest will follow.

●

21

How to Choose
Profitable New Markets

During the Middle East construction boom in the late 1970s, we decided to go to Africa instead—because there was less competition there. Africa was overlooked by most builders because they preferred to work in easier places. Businesspeople from advanced countries like the United States and Japan are discouraged by the hard living conditions in Africa and business methods that differ from other international standards. More difficult markets, however, offer the opportunity for greater profit. After studying the situation in Africa, we picked three key markets: Sudan, because it has the most land; Nigeria, because it has the biggest population; and Libya, because it has the most wealth.

Some people consider those countries risky, but the secret

of business success in such places is how well risk is managed. It's mainly a matter of being prepared, which requires continuous observation to monitor new developments. That is why I spend at least half of each year traveling abroad. By looking at, hearing, and feeling changes firsthand, it is possible to minimize risk and maximize returns.

I like to pioneer in creating new markets in Africa and other seemingly difficult places. In the three African countries we picked, there have been no big problems. We know the important people there, which is good insurance, and they know that we are working for the country. If you look ahead twenty years, the countries I selected could become big markets. The potential is there. We are not looking just for today, but for the long run. In the first stage, the first ten years in those countries, at least I didn't lose money. We developed relationships, showed we could help, and the business grew.

In Sudan, for instance, I took a long-term approach beginning in 1976. No companies from America or Japan were investing money there, but I built a tire factory, which is still the biggest industry in Sudan. The Sudanese much appreciated this plant, which saved the country foreign exchange.

Soon we found other business in Sudan. Daewoo built a hotel and a city road because the country was hosting a meeting of African heads of state. I didn't expect any big profit. We worked around the clock building that hotel, and everyone could see us under the lights. Then they had confidence in me—and our company. Sudan was short of many raw materials, which we supplied, and we buy a lot of its cotton. We built many roads with a joint-venture construction company, so we were thought of as a local company. We gave scholarships to people in Sudan. The Sudanese know Daewoo very well. The government there has been changed by a coup, but we have no problems because people know we work for the country.

In Libya, we worked very hard and got almost $10 billion in construction and trading business over ten years. If we do work that a country needs and give a very competitive price, its citizens appreciate it.

In Nigeria, we discovered that it was almost impossible to get good maintenance for automobiles. So we set up a facility to service cars within twenty-four hours and quickly made Daewoo cars a leader in the Nigerian market.

We not only did business, but helped Korea. Most of the African countries had diplomatic relations only with North Korea, but after getting to know Daewoo they have normalized diplomatic relations with South Korea.

Today in Africa you can see our construction sites in Liberia, Ghana, Nigeria, Cameroon, Gabon, Ivory Coast, Botswana, Angola—in most West African countries. Construction projects usually take about two years, so problems of lodging, communications, and transportation are first solved, and then our trading company follows.

By managing risks carefully in Africa, we've opened markets that have proved to be both durable and profitable.

But we choose them not in spite of but because of the risk.

•

No person is so worthless that he can't help someone else. And no one doesn't need help at some time.

•

Good relationships with outstanding people are more valuable than money, because you can't buy good relationships.

•

22

A Sure Way to Profit

HELP OTHERS

One rainy day, an ant got swept away by a swollen stream, but fortunately a circling dove spotted his plight. Feeling sorry for the ant, the dove dropped a leaf into the water for the ant to climb onto, and the ant was saved.

One day some time later, the dove was dozing on a tree branch. A hunter approached and took aim at him. The ant happened to be nearby, and seeing this, he bit the hunter on the foot. The hunter dropped his gun and screamed in pain, which woke up the dove, who flew away. The ant had returned the favor.

Every person needs help in one way or another at one time or another, and no person is so worthless as not to be able to help another. We are all interdependent and need one another's help.

While doing business, I have often been impressed by how very important this is. For example, when I first started Daewoo, we did some business with an Indonesian trading firm named The. At the time we were exporting fabric to The for about 17 cents per yard, but the Indonesian government suddenly put restrictions on imports and the market price of fabric there fell to about 10 cents per yard. Under a long-term contract, however, The had no way out of our contract and continued to import at the higher contract price. Knowing this, I tried to minimize The's loss by reducing its imports, but the firm was still in financial trouble. If it did not come up with $30,000, the bank was going to take it over. I went directly to The myself and handed the firm the money it needed. At the time, our company had only $10,000 in paid-in-capital, so $30,000 to us was a huge amount, and it was a tough decision to make.

Within a year, things changed dramatically. The Indonesian market opened again, and the price of fabric shot up to 36 cents per yard. Our contract was still at 17 cents per yard, which The could have legally kept to, but The offered to give me 35 cents per yard, which was only a cent lower than the market price. So we received 35 cents per yard for 17-cent-per-yard material, and we eventually made over $1 million on the deal.

So you can see how I was rewarded for the $30,000 I had given The when it was in trouble. There is always a reward for helping others. It may not always come back to the one who did the good deed, but someone will receive the benefits. This is a principle of life: to help others is to help yourself.

If you have your eye on your own profits and avoid

helping those in need, you may do all right in the short run, but in the long run it will catch up with you. If you think only of your own profit in human relations, then you are putting yourself at risk. You have to put the principle of mutual benefit to work. If one side takes everything at the expense of the other, then the relationship is not going to last very long.

At Daewoo, we always try to ensure that our partner gets as much out of a deal as we do. We have tried to impress upon people that "there's no loss in dealing with Daewoo."

The same principle applies to personal relations. If someone tries to use another person, the relationship rapidly deteriorates. For a relationship to work, it is essential for each person to empathize with the other completely, to understand his or her position and situation; only then can the relationship become a mutually beneficial one.

You can become a success in life if you have good personal relationships. Having good relations with outstanding individuals is an asset more valuable than money itself, because good relations are something you cannot buy. But human relations are as difficult as they are important, and that is another lasting principle: good things do not come easily.

One of the keys to good personal relations is mutual trust, which develops over a period of time and only with plenty of patience. Let me give you another example from my experience. When I started the company, I needed to borrow money, but I had nothing for collateral, and no one at a bank was going to lend a considerable amount to a bright-eyed young stranger. Trust had not been established. So I went to talk to the branch manager twice a week to try to persuade him to extend me a loan by explaining in detail our plans. That was the only way, but it was not working very well.

Sometimes I would go to his house early in the morning. I would pound on the door on those cold winter mornings only to be told that he was not yet up. I would stand there shivering in the cold until he came out to go to work. After about a year of this, he decided that I was credible, but it took a lot of patience on my part. We still maintain that trusting relationship.

III

GROWING

●

It is as foolish to be overly afraid of
thorns as it is to swoon over roses.

●

23

Opportunities Come from Adversity,

OR WHY CRISIS IS GOOD FOR YOU

I often tell people that the Korean War made me what I am today.

Because of the misery and hardships of the war, I got a taste of the tough life early. I learned how to develop guts to overcome fear and hardship and trials because in my early teens I was suddenly responsible for my family's livelihood.

To impress upon you that life is not easy, consider the basics of Buddhist teaching: life is suffering, and the world is a sea of it. Life is not a well-paved road, nor is it a bed of beautiful roses. Do not forget that roses have very sharp thorns.

But it is as foolish to be overly afraid of the thorns as it is just to swoon over the roses.

Success belongs to those who are not afraid of the challenge of the thorns. Just about all who are highly successful today have become that way thanks to hardship and adversity, not to a bed of roses. That is why I do not hesitate to say that the Korean War made me.

Opportunities are born out of adversity. When things are going well, everybody does well. But when everything is going well for everybody, you have to ask yourself: what makes you different, what distinguishes you from the rest?

Take, for example, a student with a good head. Since he knows he is smart, he takes it easy during his sophomore and junior years in high school, getting average grades, and he plans to cram during his senior year. He figures that if he pushes a little when he is a senior, he will have it made. But will he?

If he studies twice or three times as hard when he is a senior, he is still not going to make it. His ranking would not get any better, because all the students who studied hard previously are also studying like mad as seniors. If he does study hard, he may be able to maintain his average ranking, and that is about it. The time to do something is not when everybody else is doing it. The time to do something is when everybody else is not, when everybody else has not yet started or has stopped, when everybody else has given up. That is when success comes to someone who strives hard, who sees the opportunity that hides behind difficulties.

You have to know how to use crises. It is very interesting to take a close look at the Chinese characters used for "crisis." The first is close in meaning to the English word "risk," and the second represents chance or opportunity. So this word "risk-chance" is an ambivalent one, since it carries both negative and positive connotations. It hints at the possibility of moving in either of two different directions. A "risk-chance" can lead to either a plus or minus situation.

A pessimistic person will consider a "risk-chance" negatively and fall into despair over it; an optimistic, aggressive person will begin to dig into the same situation with hope, confidence, and the spirit of challenge and adventure. The optimistic person sees the chance or opportunity that arises in a crisis. He or she may succeed or may fail, but will at least not fear the situation; the optimist will challenge it and act, which I consider to be the wiser of the two options.

You have the right to fail as long as you have tried your best. If you just go on doing the work that you are told to do, you may not have any worries, but you will never really accomplish anything great. If a person never tastes failure, how can he or she expect to taste success?

•

What you are doing is important,
but not as important as how you go
about it.

•

24

Strive to Be Best

aving fled Seoul during the Korean War, we lived as refugees in Taegu. My father had been kidnapped and taken north, and my older brothers were serving in the army. It was up to me, at the age of fourteen, to earn a livelihood for the rest of the family. There was not much that a fourteen-year-old could do in the chaos of the war, but fortunately one of my father's former students, who worked at a newspaper, arranged for me to sell newspapers.

I usually sold the papers to the shops in the crowded Pangchon market in Taegu. As soon as I got the papers I ran to the market. If I lost time selling a couple of papers on the way, I could lose the market to other paperboys. So I was always the first one at the market, but I still could not capture the whole market, because I lost valuable time giving change as I sold to people in the first third of the market. During those precious moments, the other newsboys would catch up and pass me, securing the rest of the market for themselves.

In order to feed my family, I had to sell a minimum of one hundred papers a day; my mother and two younger brothers were always anxiously waiting for me at home. I had to come up with a new method to sell more papers, so every day before I started I would make sure I had plenty of change ready. I was able to save important time by tossing the folded bills of change with the paper, grabbing the money, and running to the next shop. In that way, I eventually was able to capture about two-thirds of the market. But the other kids were still catching up with me.

I had to improve my tactics, and I did. I just ran through the market tossing the papers to the shops—nobody could catch up with me. Then I could take my time making my way back through the market to collect the money. Not everybody paid each day, but I was able to sell all my papers and usually was able to collect what was owed me within a couple of days. After about two months, the other paperboys had given up completely, and I had the market all to myself.

People who want to become the best try their very best. If you try your best, you may not always come out on top, but you will come close to it. On the other hand, if you think that you cannot do it, that you do not have the capabilities, then you will never accomplish anything. What you are doing is important, but not as important as how you go about it; your attitude should be one of becoming the best in whatever it is you are doing. I believe that everyone who is number one in his field got there because he aimed high and tried his best. Halfhearted efforts never put anyone in a top position.

Many years ago a Hungarian soccer star was interviewed after his team captured first place in a European competition. One of the reporters asked his secret to success. He said that whenever he had time, he kicked a soccer ball; when he was not kicking a soccer ball, he was talking about soccer; and when he was not talking about soccer, he was thinking about it.

A lot of people talk about the Daewoo "miracle," but to us there was no miracle—we just worked harder and tried to become the best in our field. I am never satisfied with present accomplishments, and I will never stop striving for greater heights, because I realize that trying your best in everything you do is the only way to avoid regrets.

●

The most valuable commodity in the world is time. Like an arrow shot from a bow, it never returns.

●

25

How to Make the Most of Your Time

There are a lot of valuable things in this world: property, possessions, work, and so forth. But the most valuable thing is time. Like an arrow shot from a bow, it never returns.

"Now" lasts only for an instant; by the time you have said "now," that now has already passed and you will never be able to catch it again. That is the nature of time. You can always get another job and you can always get new possessions, but you can never recapture time.

Young people easily forget the value of time. Being young means that you have a lot of time ahead, so you might think that there is nothing wrong with wasting a little time. That is not the case.

A long time ago at Daewoo, we came up with a slogan that

typifies the Daewoo spirit: "We spare time but we don't spare sweat and effort." We know all too well the meaning and importance of time.

Success and failure depend entirely on how you spend your time. Perhaps two people may succeed at the same thing, but of the two, the person who uses time wisely will be more successful.

Days are too short for me. I wish they were thirty or forty hours long. And because time is so important to me, I sometimes shave and wash with a towel in the car on the way to work. I even occasionally have breakfast in the car.

I spend a lot of time traveling internationally, so much time that if *The Guinness Book of Records* had a section on time spent traveling, I am sure I would be listed. I am particularly sensitive about plane transfers in my travels, because I hate to waste time; a wrong connection can mean loss of an entire day or two. Whenever possible, I take night flights to reduce the amount of time wasted. I get what sleep I need on the plane, and wake up for the morning arrival fresh and ready to keep my appointments. I read on the plane, review reports from branch offices, and approve plans.

We have a tradition at Daewoo of not having meetings during work hours. We hold meetings either before or after work. By doing this, it is easy for me to meet managers at about 7:00 A.M. I have heard that employees jokingly refer to such morning meetings as "the sunrise prayer service"!

A great deal of the driving force that propelled Daewoo into what it is today is our respect for and use of time. Although we began relatively late in comparison to Korea's other conglomerates, our greatest assets were youth and time. Because we were young, we were creative, determined, and oriented toward international expansion.

A lot of people refer to our spectacular growth over the last twenty-five years as a miracle, but some are skeptical. I tell such people that we do not calculate in terms of twenty-five years. We actually worked double the time of other companies: instead of working the conventional 9:00 to 5:00, we worked from 5:00 A.M. until 9:00 P.M.

I still remember the early days at Daewoo when there was a nationwide midnight-to-4:00 A.M. curfew. We often had meetings after work that lasted well into the night, so we wound up sleeping in nearby inns. Any company that worked as hard as we did could accomplish the same thing; if it did not, there would be something wrong somewhere.

The day is twenty-four hours long for everybody. The difference lies in how you utilize those twenty-four hours. If a person works or studies three times longer than another person in a single day, then he or she is three days ahead of the other person. Of course, more important than the actual time volume is the quality of productive time in terms of the person's life.

The Roman philosopher and statesman Seneca once evaluated the use of time. He said that life was sufficiently long if you used your time effectively to accomplish something great. But if you wasted life in dissipation and laziness, and did not live for something worthwhile, you would realize that it was already too late. As he put it, life is not short by nature, but we make it short by wasting time. Somebody can amass a fortune, but if he or she is not careful with it, it can be lost in an instant.

Another person may have comparatively little, but if he or she is careful with it, it can be maintained and its value can even increase. The same principle applies to time.

Life is too precious to waste. Do not take even a moment for granted, for things are built upon the accumulation of moments.

•

Every person has infinite capabilities; the only difference between a wizard and an ordinary person is that the wizard uses more of his or her latent capabilities—and works harder.

•

26

How to Become a
Wizard

T here is a wizard who can leap over a hundred-meter-high pole whenever he wants to. He is a source of both marvel and envy, and it makes us wonder if we could ever have such powers. We wonder if his power was just tossed to him out of the blue one day while he was meditating.

At first, this wizard could not jump any farther than most of us, perhaps a meter or so. But he set a goal to leap over a hundred-meter-high pole, and he practiced every day, getting better little by little. He devoted all of his time to this one effort. Perhaps he trained himself by leaping over millet stalks that grew taller day by day. Maybe that was how he became a wizard, a specialist, an expert in his field.

It is easy to have the misconception that wizards were

born that way. But if that were the case, then experts would be born experts and chairmen would be born chairmen. But experts and chairmen were not born that way—they just worked harder at becoming professional, just like the wizard.

Each person has infinite capabilities, and the only difference between wizards and ordinary people is that wizards use their latent capabilities and work harder at whatever they are doing.

It is not very humble of me to say so, but I have been given the nickname Wizard. Perhaps I am called this because I often talk about that leaping wizard I mentioned. But the name was given to me by those around me, I think, because I have the unrelenting desire to become an expert at everything I get involved in. I must admit that I do not dislike the name. All my life I have wanted to be an expert, a specialist.

I majored in economics in college, but my first job was in an unrelated area: textiles. After ten years at it, I had become a textile wizard. Although I left the textile field some time ago, even today I can feel a piece of cloth and tell exactly what kind of product it is for, the materials that went into its production, and the production processes involved. And I am still a wizard when it comes to matching color and texture combinations.

But my wizardry is not limited just to textiles. As business began to expand, I worked hard at becoming an expert in many fields—machinery, automobiles, finance, shipbuilding, and even hotels. I made it a point to become an expert in each of these fields, and this expertise made it possible to extend existing business areas and to expand into new business areas.

As a result of all these efforts in various fields, I have gradually become an expert in management as well. When I talk with the executives under me, I can tell immediately from their facial and verbal behavior how well they have researched their respective areas. With only one or two questions I can determine the extent of their expertise.

We are living in a time of specialization. Things are changing on a daily basis; life is becoming more complicated and diversified, and the need for specialists is becoming apparent in more and more areas. Things have gradually changed from the time when one person could handle everything. Even if one person could physically handle both the volume and details of all the work, time would not permit him or her to do so. The result has been development of a highly specialized division of labor that has greatly increased efficiency. As a result, we now require experts in every field. So in today's world you have to become a total expert in your chosen field.

This does not mean that you should ignore everything else in favor of your chosen field. You need a variety of interests and a lot of good common sense. You have to be, in addition to an expert, well-rounded. The world is a big place, and life is filled with diversity. If you confine yourself to your own little world, you become like a frog confined to a well, unaware of the rest of the world around you.

I am concerned nowadays that we are so busy digging a wide well as quickly as possible that we have forgotten about the depth. Yet, to dig deep enough, you need a wide enough plot of land before you start to dig. If you really want to dig deep, at first you have to dig broadly. If you think only of the depth, it may seem on the first full shovel that you will be able to dig quite deeply; but just dig a bit deeper, and you find that you cannot get down any farther without the necessary breadth. So give yourself plenty of room before you start to dig.

A person majoring in microbiology does not have to become an expert in methods of airplane wing assembly. But whether your major is microbiology, medicine, or literature, you still need a certain breadth of general knowledge. I am talking about being cultured and well versed, which guarantees certain depth in your specialty. You need a broad understanding of such things as philosophy, etiquette, and ethics.

Today power and prestige are not guaranteed separately; that era has passed. Power today comes from being a specialist. Prestige and recognition now come from being the only person who can do a certain job.

Why are doctors respected? My observation is that they have always received respect and recognition because they are specialists.

Why are such authors as Dostoevsky, Camus, and Kafka still remembered? Because they were specialists in literature, and reached heights in literature that others did not. They are all people who did something that other people could not do, or did not do.

So become a specialist, an expert, a wizard; try to become the very best in your field, no matter what it is. And if you are wondering how to go about it, let me advise you that you should immerse yourself completely in whatever it is. Ideas, wisdom, and perception are given to those who pour themselves into something totally. To take a rest from your efforts for a while in order to get a fresh idea is foolishness.

Writing comes from the end of a pen, and you have to write and write in order to get ideas. In the same way, creative ideas and perceptions in other fields also come from immersion. Genius depends 99 percent on effort, and to become a genius in your field you have to immerse yourself.

●

You will always see more of what
you have in mind.

●

27

An Exercise for Building Your Self-confidence

S elf-confidence helps make almost anything possible, so I once devised a little exercise to build up my confidence. On the way to the office in the morning, I would add up numbers on the license plates of cars. At first I did this to improve my math ability. Later I decided that if the sum of the numbers on most license plates included the number nine, an auspicious number in the Orient, that meant good luck. On mornings that I got lots of totals of nine, nineteen, twenty-nine, or thirty-nine, I felt more confident about business that day. But I felt less confident if there were more totals with the number three. Sometimes I would tell the driver to drive around awhile until I found more license plates with nine in their totals. Then I felt confidence.

Adding numbers to look for nine may seem like a form of superstition, but you will always see more nines if you have nines in mind. We all have the power to change our destiny.

●

*When I see others sweating in a
health club, I wonder if they're
doing it because they don't have any
place else to sweat.*

●

*The object of being an entrepreneur
is not to become fat.*

●

28

My Secret Formula for Good Health

Some people evidently think that I have a secret to good health, since I'm always on the go at a pace that most people would find exhausting. It may be a bit audacious of me, but I always think of myself as being young, and I've never really had to be concerned about my health.

During the Korean War, I'd walk about six miles a day selling newspapers. Perhaps that set a good foundation for my health.

Maybe some people think that because I'm a businessman I must be a good golfer, but I've never even picked up a golf club. I certainly never had the time to take up golf, and I never considered it a useful form of exercise. So it was a great pleasure for me to discover in his book that Japan's great entrepreneur Toko Toshio felt the same way about golf. Once, some of his staff invited him out to play a round. He told them that he couldn't understand how they could be captivated by putting a ball into a small hole. He felt that running a company was infinitely more exciting.

That's exactly how I feel. Golf is at the bottom of my list; the joy and accomplishment I derive from work are infinitely greater. I can't find any health reasons for playing golf either. The exercise I get by working is so much more effective. My theory is that someone who works hard doesn't need any other exercise.

When I see others sweating in a health club, I wonder if they're doing it because they don't have any place else to sweat. I still can't comprehend why people have to spend extra time and money to stay in good shape.

If somebody asked for my secret to good health, I would have to answer, "Hard work." I get all kinds of energy when I work; yet I can understand how tedious, tiresome work can be detrimental to health. But work you enjoy begets more energy, so put joy into your work and you'll really feel alive. Sweating at work is better for you than sweating at the health club, and it's my shortcut to good health. I've said that work is my hobby, and I guess that I can also say that work is my way to stay in shape.

I think another great aid to good health is the ability to eat anything—and eat it well. I have a balanced diet, and I tend to eat lots and eat quickly. If you work hard, you have to eat a lot, and since I've been all over the world, I've gotten used to eating just about everything.

There's an old saying that food is the best preventive

medicine. If you're fussy about food, then you'll never make it internationally. To get along with others, you have to eat their food. If you go to Africa, you have to eat African food; if you go to the Middle East, you have to eat lamb. (We Koreans never eat lamb!) Even if the food doesn't appeal to you, eat it and even try to enjoy it. That's how you'll make friends.

This becomes even more important if you're trying to sell a product. There are times when you may have back-to-back dinner appointments in the same evening. Even when that happens, I make the most of both meals. I've never really been fussy about food, and I suspect that my ability to enjoy all kinds of meals with all kinds of people has contributed to my international success.

I realize that I shouldn't urge others to eat as quickly as I do. But because I've always been on the go, eating quickly has become second nature to me. Often enough, when I eat with Daewoo people I'm finished before they're even halfway through. There's a story about how Napoleon never took more than eight minutes for lunch and twelve minutes for supper. I guess that goes to show that throughout history people who have a lot to do don't spend much time on their meals.

To maintain good health you don't have to take herbal brews, go to the health club, or have some kind of extra exercise. My philosophy of good health is that it can easily be maintained by healthy daily routines and attitudes.

A really healthy person achieves a good balance between physical and mental health. Thinking that a muscular body is the key to good health can actually become an illness in itself; it could eventually lead you into the world where fists have top priority, and that can ruin your life. A healthy body is of true value only when it matches a mind that is equally healthy and upright.

Although I'm an entrepreneur, I really believe that the psychological is more important than the material. The object of being an entrepreneur is not to become fat. We should reject trends of material and economic development that lead only to self-gratification and fat stomachs. Materialism is fine as long as psychological development is equally rich and abundant.

Nowadays there are too many people who look physically fit but are mentally unfit. And if you're not fit mentally, what's the use of being fit physically? What good is a full stomach with an empty or distorted mind?

•

*There is nowhere in the world that
is not worth a trip.*

•

29

Four Ways to Find Your Greatest Teacher

Experience is a great teacher. Through experience you learn the truths of life; through experience you mature.

I read a book by the eighteenth-century British politician Philip Stanhope, Lord Chesterfield, a compilation of letters that he wrote to his son from The Hague while serving as ambassador to the Netherlands. In one of these letters he told his son that society was the greatest book of all, and that he could learn more from society than he could from all the books ever printed. Experience is the most direct and effective way of learning about society.

All the British empiricists from Francis Bacon to John Locke and David Hume argue that all of our knowledge comes from experience. In other words, we are born with a clean slate, and what we become after that is all the result of our experience. Even Confucius said that if he walked with two others, at least one of them would be a teacher to him.

I started to learn about society early because I had to make a living for the family while we were refugees in Taegu. I was able to learn the ins and outs of human relations during that period, as well as quite a bit about money and business, competition and victory, and other facts of life. Those early experiences have had a great effect on the rest of my life.

Aside from the morally reprehensible, there is nothing that you should not experience. Play hard at sports, study hard, make as many friends as possible, and fall in love. Try using a shovel, learn to drive, and go mountain climbing. Experiencing something once is better than not experiencing it at all, because you have to experience something to really know it.

Based on my experiences here's some advice. First of all, whenever you have time, travel. Traveling opens up new worlds for you if you have the proper attitude. Do not travel just to have fun; travel is a waste of time if you do not learn something from each trip. Be attentive all the time and take notice of everything carefully. Notice what is different about the place compared to other places you have been, and learn the peculiarities of each place. Just glancing is not enough. You have to take in everything beyond the superficialities, and curiosity has to be an essential part of your luggage. There is no place that is not worth a trip, although some places are better to go to—places of historical importance, for example, or prominent cultural centers.

I owe a lot to my family. I feel particularly bad because since I spend almost two thirds of the year abroad on business,

I have not had the time to be a regular father to my children. To compensate for that in a small way, I occasionally send my kids abroad during school vacation. Of course, there are educational reasons for this, too, because I want my children to become international. However, I do not send them on fun trips; that is a waste of time and money. I make sure that they travel not to current centers of Western civilization but to places like Egypt, India, and Mayan sites so that they can learn about the history of civilization and the great wisdom of mankind.

Second, I suggest that you make all kinds of friends. Making good friends is as important as travel. A broad range of friends is a great asset; a broad variety of relationships can be of great help to you in society, and you never know who your friends may become in the future.

In the process, however, remember one thing: Do not sacrifice the depth of friendship for numbers. A hundred acquaintances are useless if you do not have a close friend, a really close friend. Acquaintances may turn their backs on you in time of need, but a close friend will not.

Third, do everything with determination. If you look around, you will discover that every single thing can be a great teacher and every place is a school where you have something to learn. For example, you can even learn current fashion trends in window displays as you walk down the street. Sitting in a fog on a bus or a subway shows a lack of determination. If you have real determination, you can be creative wherever you are. Listen to a foreign-language tape while you travel around town.

Fourth, always have a book handy, for books are indirect

experiences for you. Because of the limits of time and space, we cannot experience everything directly in one lifetime; but we have plenty to learn from the experiences of others, experiences that we may never encounter. Of course, our own direct experiences are much more real to us, but we are limited, so we have to give credence to the experience of others.

Read books as you make friends—on a broad scale. Just flipping through books is like making lots of friends but no close ones, so make sure that you read intensely. Read each book with the same regard that you have for a good friend. Just skimming through even a hundred books is useless. Always have a good book on hand for when you have free time.

•

If you share the benefits of any
transaction, you will get more
business over the long run.

•

30

Six Keys to Success in Starting a Business Career

There are many different ways to succeed in business if you are creative. Someone with a new idea can be successful immediately if, for example, he or she creates a new technology or a new way of marketing. If you go through the normal systems and do things in the established ways, it will take a long time.

Here's my advice to a person setting out in business:

1. From the beginning, you have to work hard. Nothing comes without effort. If you accumulate small successes, you will gain confidence—and can see that everything is possible.

2. Small innovations are important. Even if your first job is just filling out forms, you can discover ways to do it more

efficiently. At home, you can change the furniture around every season and make it look almost as if you have a new house. You don't have to make a big invention to succeed, but can just improve many small things. You might find a new way of distributing newspapers to homes, or start a specialty store that is a little different from other retailers. Large innovations are the result of accumulating many small innovations.

3. Work for others, not just for yourself. This is a kind of insurance. If you work for a hundred others, my experience is that it is returned manyfold. The hundred things that you do to help someone else eventually becomes a thousand things done for you. If you share the benefits of any transaction, you will get more business over the long run. Since my youth, I always have worked for others. My three brothers studied in the United States, but I stayed home to look after our mother. And when I joined a company, I worked for it more than for my own company. My bosses were very happy, and I gained experience, which gave me more confidence. When I started my own company, I worked for the employees—coming in earlier than anyone else and serving as a model.

4. Avoid worrying too much about your personal net worth. I have never counted how much money I have. The reason is that I'm confident of being able to make money anytime. The secret is: hard work. So why should I count? In the future, rather than for my wealth, I would like to be known for my achievements. If you are an entrepreneur, whenever you concentrate on counting your net worth, you have reached your limit. It means you have less confidence in the future. You're not thinking enough about the business, and the company goes down.

5. Everything is possible if you have confidence. Whatever trouble arises, there is always a way to correct it. Most people think they are rising to every challenge, but are not. The average person uses only about 10 percent of his or her capabilities.

6. Potential opportunities are unlimited, but you cannot see those possibilities without working hard. Thinking is also hard work, and it will lead you to create new things.

•

*If you have the capability to be a
great musician, don't sit around
and whine that you will never be a
great painter.*

•

31

Just Visualize What You Want to Accomplish

N
ot too long ago, I invited an internationally renowned evangelist, the Reverend Robert Schuller,
to speak to our managers during a training ses-
sion. He told the managers that to become what
they really wanted, they should develop confidence through
their imagination. In other words, you can create your own
future through the powers of your mind. If you feel inferior to
others, if you think negatively and consider yourself just ordinary, then that is what you become. But if you consider yourself a notch above others, if you consider yourself successful
and superior, and live with confidence, then that is what you
become. If you want to become an outstanding violinist or
lawyer, then visualize yourself being one already.

Even when I was very young, I wanted to become a

successful businessman. Although at the time my thoughts were rather vague, I always carried this dream with me. I wanted to become an outstanding businessman who made a great contribution to the prosperity and development of the nation. Once my late father encouraged me by saying that I would make a good businessman. From then on I always visualized myself becoming one. I told myself that I wanted to become one, that I would become one, that I was one, and this belief gave me confidence made of steel.

I felt that I could accomplish anything that I started. All I had to do was make up my mind and I could do it. That fearless confidence was my only weapon when I had nothing else as a youth. And I must admit that it was the greatest, most effective weapon that I could have had.

The great Japanese entrepreneur Toko Toshio once said something important about confidence and tenacity. He said that to succeed in something, you have to have capability—but that capability alone is insufficient. You also have to have drive, concentration, and perseverance. That is what he called tenacity. Work brings with it difficulties and failures, and he said that tenacity is the ability to challenge adversity and not to flinch at failure. Disappointment and failure come with even your most creative work, but it is important to make up your mind to see your work, whatever it is, through to the end. Nothing is impossible; it is only your lack of tenacity that makes it seem impossible.

Possibilities are hiding in every area, and it is up to you to discover them. Life opens its doors to those who are positive, those who have confidence and faith, those who challenge life with energy. Robert Schuller said, "Everything we have today was at one time considered impossible." If people had continued to consider these things impossible, today we would not have penicillin or airplanes or countless other things that we now take for granted. All of these things were made possible because people had faith and confidence in themselves, and such people continue to mold world history.

But people who are negative and small-minded and who give up easily will never accomplish anything. All the doors to life are closed to them. Though such people have the capabilities to act positively, they do not realize it and continue with their simple ways. Nothing could be a greater waste of time and energy than someone who has the capabilities to become a great musician neglecting those talents and sitting around whining that he or she does not have the ability to become a great painter.

I believe that people are born with tremendous capabilities and that they were created to use those capabilities. Not using those capabilities is a waste not only for the individual, but for society as well. Visualize whatever it is you want to do, and you can do it if you put your mind to it.

●

*In true competition, there is no end
that can justify unfair means.*

●

32

How to View Your Competitors

We are living in a time of intense competition, so intense that life itself has become competition. If you are not in the front of the race, you lose: there is only one gold medal.

Every sport has regulations, and every athlete has to be well aware of them. When an athlete breaks the rules, he or she is penalized—given a warning, or even ostracized.

Daewoo has a professional soccer team, the Daewoo Royals, and a couple of years ago I was elected chairman of the Korea Soccer Association. In soccer, it is against the rules for any player except the goalkeeper to handle the ball, and for anyone to trip or block another player. Fair play is essential.

Life, like soccer, has its rules and regulations. We are all athletes in the game of life. We have to compete, and we have

---

to play fair; otherwise, the game becomes meaningless. The most important thing in the game of life is to be a clean, fair competitor. This is even more important than winning itself. A clean loss is better than a dirty victory. We have always favored a fair player over someone who will do anything just to win.

Even though we are living in an age of intense competition, we should not wind up in conflict and isolation. The object of competition is not to slay or eliminate the opponent. Competition should be something that makes life better for all the participants; a true competitor can be even better for you than a friend or a teacher.

Take the marathon, for example. Records are not broken by people running alone. New records are set when a runner has someone to pace himself or herself with, someone to compete with. When one runner passes another, the second is stimulated to try harder to pass the first. This continues, and both runners often end up with better times.

When competition causes conflict and isolates individuals, however, it loses its purpose and creative energy. It destroys not only individuals but the basis of common good and common prosperity as well. Competing only for yourself and running others into the ground in the process is actually a form of self-destruction.

You cannot live for yourself and by yourself. You have to cooperate, and you have to serve others. Take, for example, the automotive industry, which relies heavily on the machine and component industries. It is impossible for one corporation to put a car on the market by itself. A single car is the result of thousands of components made by a broad variety of production firms. In the same way, we are infinitely dependent on one another for everything in our lives.

Companies compete fiercely to produce a better product. As a result of this, quality improves for the consumer. If there were only one manufacturer, the quality and technology probably would not improve very much; for example, we might still be using manual washing machines. Of course, the costs in time and money to achieve high quality and technological superiority can sometimes be astronomical, but companies are willing to make these commitments to come up with a better product and to outdo their competitors.

But there are companies which, taking competition too far, use devious means. They start rumors about competitors and try to devise schemes to block international joint ventures or technical license agreements by their competitors. This is where the true meaning and the spirit of fair play are lost.

You have all heard the phrase "The end justifies the means," but in true competition there is no end that can justify unfair means. Not playing fair is a violation of the principles of true competition. Those who play fair are the ultimate victors.

●

There should never be a time for you to think or say, "I've finally made it!"

●

33

The Dangers of Complacency

Youth is filled with the spirit of challenging the status quo and with the adventure of trying the impossible. This is what makes youth worthwhile, and that spirit guarantees youthfulness.

Youth has no fear of failure. People who fear failure and who are content with the status quo have lost their youth, no matter what age they may be. Yet people who act young, people who are filled with the spirit of challenge and adventure for the future, are young regardless of their age.

Young people create the world of tomorrow, by shaping that tomorrow through their spirit of challenge and adventure. Because they have nothing to look back on, they look to the future; since they have nothing to look down on, they look up. They have nothing to lose, so they have no anxieties. Because they are young, they know no danger and they are filled with vitality. If they forfeit adventure for stability and refuse to challenge the status quo, they are losing their youth. Young people think of a future full of gains and achievements, and they have no time to worry about possible losses or failures. Thinking of tranquillity and comfort and merely maintaining the status quo are signs of fading youth.

It is natural for new company recruits to be overflowing with determination and enthusiasm for their work. They have to invest their youth to create a brighter tomorrow; they have to study hard, challenge, and develop themselves. The results of their efforts are promotion and an increase in assets. Those are the natural rewards of investing youthful vitality.

I see some instances, however, where those lively youths become complacent once they reach the executive level. They stop studying, stop challenging, and lose interest in developing themselves. They get into the suitability syndrome and seem concerned mainly with preserving the assets that they have accumulated. They think they have made it, so they do a suitable amount of work, conduct themselves properly, and take a sufficient amount of relaxation. It is really too bad that they do not seem to be aware that they are dooming themselves through complacency.

There should never be a time for you to think or say, "I've finally made it!" Feeling satisfied that you have reached your goal is the most dangerous moment of all. If you have reached one goal, then you have to set a higher goal. You have to think in terms of never really having reached your final goals.

Movement is the condition of life, and activity is proof

that you are alive. The lifeless do not move; if you do not move, you remain static.

There is no hope when youth has lost its spirit of challenge and adventure. This is true on the personal, corporate, and collective levels. A lack of vitality spells death. When youthful vitality and hope are lost, again whether on the personal, corporate, collective, or national level, then the only thing to do is to prepare for a funeral.

You will notice some individuals and some companies age rapidly. Once I met the president of a small component manufacturing firm. I was rather startled to find out that the president knew nothing about his products. The factory manager had to explain everything to me. Well, I let that pass. But I started feeling sad when I noticed that the president's car was much larger and finer than my car. It made me realize that I could not stake anything in the future of his company because the company president was completely absorbed by the comforts of the present and had no visions of the future. He was complacent. I have always perceived that contentment and complacency signal the end of everything.

●

An empty waterwheel is quite noisy,
but a full one is quiet and has no
need for noise.

●

34

Advice to Youth

After dining at a restaurant, many foreigners will ask the waitress for a "doggie bag" so that they can take the leftovers home. But we Koreans do not do this, no matter how expensive the meal may be. To us, asking for the leftovers seems a bit awkward and we cannot bring ourselves to do it, as if in some way it was going to reflect badly on us. We are afraid that others might think that we are either very poor or very cheap.

But what does it mean to foreigners? Does it mean that they are cheapskates, that they are poor? Is it something that will reflect badly on them?

It seems to me that we are too hung up on exterior impressions. We like to put up fronts. People who do not know much like to pretend they are scholarly, and people with little to spare often throw money around just to impress others. A lot of us sacrifice inner beauty for outer appearance. We think we have to talk big to impress others, and a lot of us with nothing on the inside flaunt the exterior. We call it "fancy outside, empty inside."

But I hope that young people will not fall for this type of behavior. Do not waste your lives by selling your exterior. Youth is the time of life when you have to devote yourself to inner development. Real worth and real style cannot come from your exterior; they are things that have to come from within. Exterior style is frivolity, but real style that comes from within is lofty, and such subtle style is eternal. An empty waterwheel is quite noisy, but a full one is quiet and has no need for noise.

Young people are sensitive by nature, and because of this sensitivity it is easy to fall into this trap of living for and by exterior impressions. That is why a lot of singers and actors wind up competing with one another in clothing. Many young people are attracted to entertainers through their flamboyant packaging. This then leads to fads, and eventually to gossip about the entertainers without their even knowing it.

I am not saying that it is bad to like certain songs or certain stars. But youth is a very important time of life, too short a period to waste on fleeting fads. I really think that youth is the time of life when you should devote yourself to developing inner strength and style.

Our first project in Sudan was the Presidential Guest House, and it was to be built right across from the Presidential Mansion. The Sudanese government was not particularly interested in dealing with us, perhaps because North Korea was already building a youth center in Sudan. In addition, the Sudanese government had diplomatic relations with North Korea, but not with South Korea. Overall we were in a difficult position.

I felt, however, that if we let this opportunity go by, we would never be able to enter the Sudanese market. I made up my mind to work my way—rather than talk my way—into the market. Why? Because I believe that a single action is much more impressive than unlimited talk. So we worked on the guest house around the clock, and no doubt those night lights did not go unnoticed across the street at the Presidential Mansion. We worked like mad, and we finished way ahead of schedule. The president probably compared our work with that of the North Koreans, and we greatly impressed him with both our progress and our technology. So we opened the door to both diplomatic and trade relations with Sudan.

Talk is not the most powerful method of persuasion. Talk is important, and you have to be able to talk well and talk sincerely. You have to be able to impress others with your thoughts. But actions really move people. Talk can fail, but actions know no failure. If you really want someone to believe you and to believe in you, then you have to act sincerely and convincingly.

Great inner strength also signifies real ability. The people we really need in this world are not the ones who stand around looking good; we need people with real abilities. They may not brag and boast, but they are greatly welcomed wherever they go. People do not really believe those who live by their packaging and have no abilities.

●

*A frog in a well has no
comprehension of the vastness of the
world around him.*

●

35

The World Is Yours

I first became aware of the great importance of technological development when we took over the Korea Machinery Company in 1976. Since technological development would determine the success of the company, I decided to send some people to M.A.N. of Germany for technical training. At Daewoo, we already had a technical license agreement with M.A.N., so I selected twelve managers and assistant managers, all engineering graduates, for foreign training.

However, there was resistance to this, particularly from those in charge of production. They felt that the loss of twelve key personnel would seriously affect productivity. They were, of course, sincerely concerned for the company. But I felt that it was necessary to think of long-term benefits rather than short-term priorities. I felt that we could not steer the company into the future without technological development, so I convinced the people that short-term deprivations were actually an investment in long-term growth.

When the twelve engineers returned from Germany after a year, the production personnel could see that I had been right: the technology that the engineers had absorbed during the year brought our standards up by at least five years.

Above all, you have to be future-oriented. There are people who are fixed on the past, who always are saying, "In the old days, I used to . . ." Those people are blinded by the past and have no vision of the future. Being fixated on the past or satisfied with the comforts of today deprives you of visions for tomorrow.

A frog in a well has no comprehension of the vastness of the world around him. The higher the mountain you climb, the broader the vista; the higher a bird flies, the broader and more expansive the world. Getting out to see this immense world broadens your vision and helps you to overcome selfishness and egocentricity.

From the very start, the world was my focal point. While the domestic market is limited, the international market is limitless. I made Daewoo grow by removing borders and barriers to that limitless market. From the beginning, we gave preferential hiring to those who were willing to challenge the world, who wanted to create a new world, and who were internationally oriented, because they represented the Daewoo spirit.

•

Life really begins with meeting.

•

36

People Who Influenced Me Most

Martin Buber once said something to the effect that life really begins with meeting. I can understand fully what he meant by that. I really believe that the direction and quality of your life can be influenced greatly by those you meet.

The people you meet when you are young can influence your entire future. It is essential for you to follow the example of people you respect. Perhaps that is why we put pictures of such people on our desks or walls. Just think of the difference in the future of a person who follows the example of a pessimistic philosopher such as Arthur Schopenhauer and the future of a person who follows the example of men who had a pure love for freedom and values, like Mahatma Gandhi or Abraham Lincoln.

I have met countless people in my life, including really outstanding people, as well as people I did not really care to meet. Some faces are still very vivid in my mind, while I have easily forgotten other faces. One thing is definite, however: much of what I am today is the result of meaningful meetings I have had with certain people, the people whom I remember the most. So let me mention them here.

My mother was an outstanding person.

Of course, most people respect their mothers, but I am particularly proud of mine. My father had been a highly respected educator and provincial governor, but he, as I have told, was captured and taken north during the Korean War. The difficulties my mother had in raising five children by herself were immense, but she managed to put us all through college. Her life was, simply, total sacrifice for her children. The core of my corporate philosophy is sacrifice, and I must admit that it is due largely to my mother's influence on me.

I can still vividly remember her, a devout Christian, praying or singing hymns four times a day without fail. I must say that her prayers were a source of great strength for me.

The positive Christian view of the world, of sacrifice and service, was deeply instilled in me by my mother and by my four years at Yonsei University, a Christian school. As a result, I believe that religion is important. Some people say that the time has come in the world when religion is no longer necessary. They talk as if religion were outdated and a mistake. In my opinion, however, the more uncertain and seemingly worthless the times are, the more we need a stabilizing principle from which to work.

* * *

I have a lot of close friends, and we have always helped one another. I graduated from Kyonggi High School, and when I first went to work after college, a lot of classmates as well as upperclassmen and underclassmen from Kyonggi were of great help to me.

The vice chairman of the Daewoo Group, Lee Woo-Bock, was a high school classmate. As high school juniors, we had the same homeroom. Unlike me, he was a model student. In the confusion after the Korean War, I went to the school of hard knocks and did not study for a year. So it was difficult when I went back to school. My grades were not very good, and my conduct was not anything to brag about. By the time graduation was approaching, my marks were among the highest in my class. Much of this was due to help from my lifelong friend Lee.

When I first started Daewoo and it was hard to find help, he was right there to take part. It is hard to express my gratitude for his being there at a time when I really needed some outstanding people.

I was also greatly influenced by a high school teacher, Lee Seok-Hee, who later went on to become president of Chung-Ang University and is now chairman and president of the Daewoo Foundation. He was our homeroom teacher in my junior year of high school. As I mentioned, at the time I was one of the worst students in the class, and, having recently arrived from the back alleys, I caused a lot of mischief.

I do not know what Mr. Lee's intentions were, but in the first term he appointed me vice president of the homeroom class. The next term he appointed me sergeant at arms. My life suddenly changed when I became sergeant at arms. I knew that it was important for me to set an example for the other students. Up until that time, I was not even very good at saluting the upperclassmen. All of a sudden there I was, sergeant-at-arms. Every morning I would stand before the mirror to make sure my school uniform was perfect, and I, too, began to straighten out. I began to study hard.

Mr. Lee was the first person in my life to recognize me for my latent potential and character. That is why I consider meeting him a turning point in my life. I studied hard and began to change in order to prove to him that his recognition was not groundless. If people believe in you, you try hard not to let them down.

Not all students are good students, and some are troublemakers. It is precisely those students—the ones who do not study and who make trouble—who need greater concern and attention than others. Simply yelling at them and scolding them do not work. You have to take an interest in the student and discover his or her unique capabilities. You have to recognize the student for his or her potential, and give direction in a way that will help the student realize his or her unlimited potential. Albert Einstein once failed as a student, and Thomas Edison was tossed out of school.

●

*The child plucks the fruit from a
tree the grandfather planted.*

●

37

A Lesson from the World of Spiders

There is a kind of spider that skillfully lays a large number of eggs in the bark of a tree and proceeds to disguise them with her web. After a period, the baby spiders hatch, and the mother spider, with no thought of herself, goes about the business of finding food for her babies just as all animals and insects do. When the baby spiders are strong enough to catch their own food, however, the exhausted mother dies.

Even more surprisingly, in another species of spider, the mother actually feeds herself to the babies. It seems a bit unbelievable, but the mother's body provides sufficient nutrients for the baby spiders. It is very moving to note that the life of the baby spiders depends on the sacrifice and death of their mother, that the mother has to die for the babies to live.

In the same sense, the prosperity of a future generation depends on the sacrifices made by the current generation. Indeed, there can be no prosperity without sacrifice. On a more personal level, the happiness of children depends on the sacrifices made by parents. The sweat and tears of one generation result in joy for the next. By the same token, lazy, irresponsible parents forge a trail of misery for their children.

It has been my observation that families who live well are those in which the parents have sacrificed and worked hard for the next generation rather than working for themselves. As if following the natural law of spiders, our parents tightened their belts a few notches and worked hard for us. Our prosperity today is the result of the sacrifices made by the previous generation.

This is true of every prosperous nation: prosperity is built on the sacrifices of an entire generation. People often talk about the "Miracle of the Rhine," but was it a miracle? The Miracle of the Rhine was one of hard work around the clock by an entire generation to construct a new Germany. The sound of construction was the sound of sacrifice. That sacrifice was the power behind a prosperous Germany today.

Examples abound. The pioneering spirit of sacrifice went on for generations in building American prosperity, and Japan is largely the fruit of sacrifices made during the Meiji restoration.

Nothing comes free, and nothing is accidental.

The more you dig, the deeper the hole, and the deeper the hole the more water from the well. This is what it is all about.

In Korea, the generation during the 1960s made the great

sacrifices for the future, so much so that it has even become habit for me to describe my generation as the generation of sacrifice. It was during the sixties that we opened our eyes to the possibility of constructing a strong economy and a strong nation, and we went about accomplishing that task with unmatched fervor and determination. What the younger generation has today is the fruit of those efforts and sacrifices.

I am often asked the same question by people from prosperous nations: "Why do you work so hard all the time and never even take a day off? Isn't it about time you felt a little satisfaction and took it easy?"

I always give the same reply: "You live a lot better than we do, so don't you think our next generation should close the gap a bit? My generation feels a sense of mission to set the foundation for closing that gap. It's a little premature for us to sit around feeling satisfied."

I personally feel that we still have a lot of sacrifices to make. I am concerned about the tendency of some who, with their newfound habits of lavish living, act as though they were part of an economically advanced nation. We have to recover our past sense of sacrifice and the spirit of challenging the future, since we are still living in a period that demands continued hard work. If you actually think about it from the perspective of one generation sacrificing for the next, then every generation should be making sacrifices for an even better future. No matter what its accomplishments may be, a generation should control its feelings of satisfaction; the satisfactions of one generation result in dissatisfaction in the next.

The child plucks the fruit from a tree the grandparent planted. If there is no tree, there is nothing for the child to pick. If an entire generation thinks only of itself, what will be left? Even if we are not around to pick the fruit, we have the responsibility to plant the trees. What a joy it is to think of grandchildren plucking from the tree and reflecting on what their grandparents did and why they did it!

Sacrifice is only possible when you discard all thoughts of self—when you think only of others and when you place the "greater good" above personal profit and greed. Sacrifice is the ultimate form of altruism.

IV

LEADING

•

If a boat has too many rowers, it winds up on a mountain. Too few, and it doesn't move.

•

Anyone who sees leadership as a means for personal gain does not have the credentials to be a leader.

•

38

What Makes a Leader

"Pure springs make for clean rivers" is an old Korean adage, and it is true: the upper waters have to be pure for a river to be clean. Society is the same. Leaders have to be clean for society to be clean. It is no exaggeration to say that you can assess a society by the example set by its leaders. We need leaders who inspire the citizenry with confidence, courage, and a sense of mission.

Not everyone can become a leader, but the number of leaders we have is important. In Korea, we say that if a boat has too many rowers, it winds up on a mountain; if there are too few, however, the boat does not move. It is essential that those with the qualities and capabilities of leadership become leaders. A society is headed for trouble if it does not have such people.

What makes a leader? Leaders have to have a number of

capabilities. They have to be convincing and able to organize people. Leaders must, through strong leadership, correct contradictions and inefficiency, and know how to utilize the group's energy for prosperity and development.

But leadership should not be confused with dictatorship. The leadership I am talking about is vastly different from that which goes against the group for which it is supposed to be working.

Leaders must have a thorough sense of duty. Leaders must consider their work a mandate from heaven. They must live and die for their work, their one and only mission in life. If leaders do not have such a sense, then the group becomes a mass of confusion, unable to function in a healthy manner. Someone who sees leadership as a means for personal gain does not have the credentials to be a leader.

A leader must also have an important sense of sacrifice, and that comes with a sense of mission, for the two go hand in hand. Leadership is not something that comes merely from sitting in a high position. It can come only to those who have both a sense of mission and a sense of sacrifice for the good of the group.

Becoming a leader is like walking down a road of thorns. Only those who are willing to sacrifice their private lives, the things they like—even their families—can become leaders. You can see that not everyone can become a leader; it depends on whether the person is willing or not to make such sacrifices.

In order to make Daewoo a success, I had to give up my family life. I went without sufficient sleep. I did not have time to develop a single hobby. And I have never even had time for a drink. I gave up the joys of close-knit family life for the company.

At first, my wife was filled with complaints, but she is much more accepting now, maybe because she figures that she does not have much choice. My wife is now chairman of the Seoul Hilton Hotel. And I always have to live with the fact that I have never taken my kids on a vacation. But I think they have come to appreciate the why of it, and I even think they may be a little proud of me. So I am quite fortunate, and very grateful. Of course, I know the importance of the family, and that the basis of happiness is a good family life. But a leader must at least be able to transcend private comforts and considerations. If everyone did only what he or she wanted to, who would lead?

Our personnel policy at Daewoo is based on this. We like people who are creative, who challenge, who are willing to make personal sacrifices and work hard. Those are people who have leadership qualities, people who can become Daewoo company presidents. Even if they lack creativity, we like them if they have a strong sense of accomplishment and if they try their very best.

Such people can become Daewoo executives because they put the public good above their private satisfactions, and because they consider working for social and economic development more important than their social standing. The people who led Daewoo to success have traded their private comforts and joys for a much greater satisfaction.

On the other hand, there are people who work only for their own profit and happiness. They are more satisfied with a happy personal and family life than with the satisfaction that comes from leading development and success. These people never make it beyond the manager level. The people we really do not have any use for at Daewoo are those who cannot distinguish between work for public or private benefit; we have no need for people who confuse the two.

A person receives respect as a leader by having a true sense of mission, a sense of sacrifice, and strong values. This is where we can distinguish between leaders and dictators. People obey dictators out of fear, not out of respect. People do not fear real leaders, they respect them. Power and prestige come from respect, and a leader has to earn respect.

•

Don't be afraid to spend lots of money when needed. But never waste money, not even small amounts.

•

39

Money Is Neutral

A really smart person knows how to use both time and money wisely. So let me tell you that you should not waste even small amounts of money any more than you should waste time.

It's good to have a healthy attitude toward money from the time that you are young. Money in itself is, of course, neutral—it is neither good nor bad. What becomes good or bad is the way that you use it.

Money should be used only when it is needed, and the standard for using it is profitability—to benefit yourself and others. Spending for your own education, for medical expenses, or to help those in difficulty is money used wisely, and there is no need to be stingy about it in such cases. If you are using money properly, the amount should not matter—do not be afraid to use lots of money when necessary.

On that basis, do not waste even small amounts. Do not

use money foolishly, as you might when you have an urge to buy something you do not need. Some people will buy something just because it is cheap, not because they need it, and there are people who buy things just because others buy them—the "keeping up with the Kims" syndrome. That is pure foolishness.

When we took over the Korea Machinery Company, I decided to set up employee benefit facilities to improve motivation and develop a sense of camaraderie. At that time, in 1976, employee benefit programs were practically unheard-of in Korea. But I concluded that the time had come to pay attention to this issue. So I gave directives for employee saunas, barbershops, singles dormitories, and modern cafeteria facilities. The managers were opposed to this, for the total cost would be several million dollars, a huge amount at the time.

The managers had justifiable objections. Total capital at the company was only double the figure for the proposed facilities, and they thought that the money could be better spent on something directly related to production. Moreover, the company had been running a chronic deficit. The managers felt that the top priority should be erasing the debt, and I could not really say that they were wrong. But I did not waver. My decision was to invest the money in employee benefits first. If morale was increased, then production would naturally improve and the company would continue to grow. I had no reservations about the amount of money, as it was a wise long-term investment. This is how I operate—if something is worthwhile to me, then I do not worry about the figures. On the other hand, I can become a real Scrooge if I think money is being used unwisely.

At the time, we had commuter buses in Seoul running to and from the production site in Inchon, a distance of about twenty miles. Each bus had to pay a 500-won (about $1 at the time) highway toll. But I discovered that if the bus got off at the interchange before the plant and took the local road, we could save about 25 cents per commute each way. There was not any sense in wasting money, no matter how small the amount.

The issue here is not the several million dollars or the 25 cents. The issue is using money wisely. Spending several million dollars was just as wise as saving 25 cents.

I usually select gifts personally for our business associates, and I often choose pottery or folk-craft items. At times, the salesmen try to jack the prices way up because I am chairman of a large conglomerate. When they do, I just bargain them all the way down again, because there is no sense in wasting money. The salesmen might consider me a cheapskate, but I do not see it that way. We have to correct the thinking that someone who throws money around is really generous and someone who uses it wisely is a cheapskate.

Our Daewoo production plants do not cause much pollution, but we have no qualms about using money wisely for environmental protection facilities at plants that do. And we are not cheapskates when it comes to compensation for the family of someone who dies on the job. We just know when and how to use money properly and effectively. Someone who uses money only when it should be used is someone who really knows how to use it. Everything depends on the wisdom of the user.

●

Even the best people do not consider every possibility.

●

40

The Best Kind of Chief Executive

Several years ago I spent a few days taking the head of a big Japanese trading firm around to see Daewoo's factories, and he was surprised that I knew the details of every operation. My Japanese visitor, a well-educated gentleman, seemed a little ashamed that his knowledge about his own company was not that deep. We got to be good friends, so I told him my theory about the two kinds of business leaders. One kind of chief executive commands respect by encouraging subordinates to come up with new ideas and handle the details. That kind of chief executive is suitable for many companies.

I'm the other kind of leader, a hands-on executive. This has its dangers, of course. When employees come to me with ideas or plans on which they have worked very hard, I want to encourage and praise them, but I can always see a way to do it better. When personnel changes are made among senior managers, for instance, usually about 80 percent of the plan is good. So I move things around. I know all of our senior managers well, better than anybody else.

Similarly, managers come in and proudly explain how they are going to arrange financing for a project. Even the best people do not consider every possibility. The easiest borrowing usually has the highest rates, but shopping around and studying the possibilities harder can get you lower rates. Even when someone comes in with a plan for borrowing at a good rate, I always ask if the companies in our own group have been consulted. Some companies have surplus funds at certain times of the year and can lend them at an even better rate than the banks.

Since I've done all these things many times before, I know about them. Much as I want to encourage managers, almost always their plans can be improved, and I must tell them, "You can do better." My style of leadership may not be suitable for all companies, but it makes our people achieve more than they ever dreamed was possible.

●

*You can never be justly criticized
for making too much money, or too
little. Only for spending it unwisely.*

●

41

How to Make Money and Use It Well

When it comes to making money, I am an expert. I have the confidence at least to match the best when it comes to making money. My name has consistently been on the list of top money-makers in Korea since I started in business. And the fact that I am often listed among top entrepreneurs internationally testifies to my money-making abilities. To put it simply, I know how to make money.

Wherever I go, I immediately see where money is to be made. I once joked that every street is paved with gold—so I just rake it in. Of course, there are plenty of places in the world where the streets are not paved with money, and making money is not the easiest thing in the world to do. It requires a lot of work and plenty of hardship. Nevertheless, I made this joke to show where my real interests are.

An artist who goes to the countryside to paint scenery looks only for good scenery. Someone who goes fishing always remembers the best places to fish. In the same way, an entrepreneur looks for ways to make money wherever he goes.

Since I have a talent for making money, whenever I visit someplace new, I get inspired as to what would sell. But there is one talent that I have yet to develop, and this is one of my shortcomings: when it comes to using money, forget it.

I feel that no matter what needs to be done, it should be done by someone with a talent for it. Someone with a talent for sports should play sports, and children with a talent for music should learn music. There is no sense in trying to turn a child who is a potential musician into a talentless engineer.

Just as there are people with a talent for making money, there are people with a talent for using it. If you give it to someone without a talent for using it, there is a good chance that it will be wasted.

I have not made money around the world for myself or for my family. If I had, by now I would be a very rich man, but at the same time I would also probably feel pretty empty. I have never thought of Daewoo as being mine. I do not own Daewoo; I am a specialist in its management.

Simply, all the money I have made is not mine. I feel that the money I have made is for people with special capabilities to contribute to society. Consequently, I established the Daewoo Foundation. My true motivation for establishing the foundation, with almost all of my assets, about $37 million at the time, sprang from a firm lifelong belief that an enterprise and money should be used in such a way.

The Daewoo Foundation's main activities include conducting academic research centered on the basic sciences, and support for publishing the results. Basic sciences are essential to all knowledge and learning, and have been rather neglected in Korea. But I do not interfere with what the foundation is doing. The foundation is in charge of everything, and the people there are more talented than I am in using the money wisely and properly.

For over ten years, the foundation has been supporting medical programs in such remote Korean areas as Muju, Wando, Shinan, and Chindo. The medical staffs there are making great personal sacrifices and contributions to improve the health of people in these agricultural and fishing areas, which are fairly isolated from mainstream society and have numerous educational problems. It is a task that no one would take without a true sense of mission. The dedication of these medical staffs is even more admirable when you consider that we live in a time when the benevolent act of healing can easily be turned into a means of great personal profit.

Actually, I would like to expand the number of hospitals in such regions, but there are not enough doctors willing to make the sacrifice. So we select bright young people from these areas who have a sense of mission and support their education. When they complete their training, they can then return to their hometowns and carry on the work.

In education, the Daewoo Foundation supports schools—from kindergarten through high school—in Okpo, the site of the Daewoo Shipyard, as well as Ajou University in Suwon. Since 1978, the foundation has provided overseas training for journalists and for research publications through the Seoul Press Foundation. Such efforts provide people, who in the future will greatly influence public opinion, with opportunities to study further and broaden their horizons.

Maybe all this sounds like a lot of boasting to you. Good works are most beautiful when they are done anonymously. So it does not seem quite right for me to be telling you directly what Daewoo is doing. But I hope that you do not misunderstand, for I have not told you all of this either to brag or to be praised. I only want to give you an example of how not to be preoccupied merely with making money for yourself. And I will be satisfied if I can get across the point that using money wisely is more important than making money.

It is a mistake to do business merely to satisfy your own greed. The reason some entrepreneurs are criticized is not that they do not make enough money, or that they make too much money, but that they do not know how to use it wisely.

If you do not have a talent for using money wisely, then entrust it to someone who does. It is not at all difficult, unless you regard business and the money you make as yours and yours alone.

•

I am proud to wear a business suit.

•

42

Why Executives Should Live Below Their Means

S ome years back my wife arranged to build us a new house, but I learned about it only after the construction was completed. Though this is no luxurious mansion, the house is bigger than the one we had before, and I felt uncomfortable about living there. Even now upon arriving home, I wonder if I'm at the right place. What concerns me most is being a model for others. No one criticized me, but I didn't want to set the wrong example. A leader has to be a model for his followers. If his standard of living is too high, others will want it too.

I normally avoid staying in a hotel suite when traveling. An ordinary room is good enough, because I only sleep there. And in Third World countries I usually stay in a Daewoo staff house along with other employees—to see how they live, and to spend more time with them.

This is not just to be humble or to save money, but to show the right spirit. You should live a bit below your means. That provides a margin of safety. Once you live at a high level, of course, going down a notch is really hard.

When we first set up an office in New York, I didn't allow any of the staff to buy a car—even those who could afford it. We had one company car for business, but our people came to work on the bus or subway. They were not ashamed, but proud of it. And when those employees returned home, they did not have to lower their living standard. This is very important psychologically.

My employees who are assigned overseas get a higher salary than at home. But I don't want managers to feel unhappy about going down a step when they return, so we save 15 to 20 percent of their salary in a bank. Otherwise, almost everyone would find a way to spend it all abroad.

I had a good personal lesson on the difficulty of downgrading your standard. For years I never traveled first-class on airlines. Many friends in smaller companies would pass me on their way up to the front cabin. It made them a little uncomfortable seeing me in the back of the plane, but I was proud to do it. Then Korean Airlines gave me and the chairman of another big Korean group—just the two of us—a free pass to travel anywhere first-class because we're such big customers. So I started traveling first-class. Within a few years, other companies complained to the airline about those passes, so they were withdrawn. After flying first-class, I discovered it was really difficult returning to the back of the plane. Now I pay to fly first-class.

*　　*　　*

I'll never forget the first time I saw high society in America. The late Malcolm Forbes hosted a big party at his New Jersey home in 1987 to celebrate the seventieth anniversary of his magazine. The guests, heads of big companies from all over the United States, arrived in limousines and helicopters. Everyone wore black tie—except me. I came in a business suit, arriving with my wife in a Buick driven by the general manager of our New York office. Mr. Forbes didn't seem to mind at all, and he took me around to meet all the important people.

Frankly, I had mixed feelings about the party. In one way, I found out that this really is the United States—a big place where people come to dinner by helicopter. In another way, though, I felt it was too luxurious. I wondered how top executives could spend so much time and money to attend a party. I'm not criticizing them, but I did feel uncomfortable about the lavishness. Other guests may have thought I was a country boy, since I didn't wear a tuxedo. But I was not shy or intimidated. I was proud to come in a regular business suit.

Every man has his stature, some level that he can afford. And most people usually try to show that they can live better than that—really above their means. I feel more comfortable living at least one notch below my status.

When Daewoo had an office in the Empire State Building in the early 1970s, I used to stay nearby at a dilapidated hotel. At that time, others who really could not afford it would stay in much better hotels. In my case, staying in that hotel and walking to the office was both very convenient and economical. Instead of trying to show off by staying at a fancy place, I felt comfortable realizing that I accomplished more by staying there and doing my work very efficiently.

•

It is foolish to brag about the amount of assets you have, because that means you have nothing else to brag about.

•

A person who has amassed a fortune, but doesn't know how to use it for others, is poor, not rich.

•

Never consider your money or your possessions as your own.

•

43

Why I Work Like a Madman

There are entrepreneurs who manage a business for their own accumulation of assets, and that is their only motive. As a result, they are always on edge worrying about their worth. On the other hand, there are entrepreneurs who run a business to accomplish and only to accomplish, and they live for the joy and love of the process of accomplishing. You cannot deny that the purpose of a business is to make money, but I feel that a company should not exist for profits alone.

Just as there are companies that exist for profits and companies that exist for accomplishment, there are individuals who exist for material gain and individuals who exist for accomplishment. Which of the two individuals really lives well? I can clearly tell you one thing, and that is that people who live fixated on their own wealth will never be satisfied, because there is no end to their greed. That type of greed can move a rich person with ninety-nine things to slay another person who has only one thing, just so that the rich person can have all one hundred.

Someone who lives only for his or her own wealth can never know the true joy of life, because the nature of material greed knows no limits. Take a man who has worked hard for a long time and finally buys a house. By buying it, he has become wealthier, and he is happy for a while. But then he starts to notice bigger and better houses all around him, and the nature of human material greed is that the man will want a bigger and better house. That man will never be happy as long as he is concerned with possessions. A life filled with dissatisfaction and greed knows no joy. I really believe that the purpose of life cannot be found in the accumulation of possessions.

It is foolish to brag about the amount of assets you have, because that means you have nothing else to brag about. If there is something about assets to boast of, it should be the quality of those assets and how you use them, not the quantity. A person who has amassed a fortune and does not know how to use it for others is poor, not rich. Someone who has much less and knows how to use it for the benefit of others is the really rich person.

To take this a step further, you should never consider your money or possessions as your own. Thinking so gives birth to the personal greed to become richer and wealthier, a greed that not only knows no satisfaction but that also can eventually lead to unethical behavior.

Christianity talks about a "sense of stewardship," the sense that whatever you have during this life is not yours, but something with which you have been entrusted. This carries with it a responsibility to take care of what you have and to use it properly for others. I like this sense of stewardship.

People are limited in the sense that even if all of mankind dies, the universe will continue eternally. And what you consider to be yours forever will belong to someone else after you die. So we should be humble before the absolute laws of nature.

In another sense, possessions are the beginning of suffering and anguish. That is why Buddhism stresses nonattachment and possessionlessness as the ways to true freedom.

Although I am the executive of a huge corporation, I have no particular interest in possessions. People who think that an entrepreneur runs a corporation out of greed for possessions would never be able to understand the pure joy of accomplishment in succeeding in making a large corporation or doing big business. They would consider me—someone who thinks twenty-four-hour days are too short—some kind of a fool if I were not doing all of this for my own wealth.

But I have not worked like a madman just to make a few coins. I have been a hard-core workaholic for the joy of accomplishment. Wealth and possessions could never even begin to compare with the joy of accomplishment involved in running a corporation. What drives me to work harder and harder are such things as the joy of doing what everyone said was impossible and the joy of winning a contract with a better product on the international market. These things give meaning to my life and are the source of power behind my nonstop work.

No matter how much money you have, you could not possibly own everything—there are limits to possessions. So I do not want to be remembered as a person who made money. To me, that would be an insult rather than a compliment. It would mean that there was nothing else to say about me as a person. I want to be remembered as one who accomplished.

•

*A risky situation needs to be
watched continuously.*

•

44

Proud to Sweat It Out in Africa

The most important way of minimizing risk is to watch a changing situation continuously, which is why I'm always going to places in Africa.

In my younger days, I would bring two or three big sample bags to very hot African countries and travel over unpaved roads to their cities. I sweated so much that it looked as if I had just had a shower. But at that time I was proud to be the first Korean businessman to go to that new market. I was the first Korean businessman to go to Moscow, to Beijing, to Ho Chi Minh City, and to many other places.

Once I went to Angola, and at my hotel the breakfast buffet was black—from all the flies on the food. I couldn't eat it at first. I ordered only eggs in the shell and bought fruit in the market to cut open myself. But I was always hungry. After two or three days, I began eating from the buffet. While other people don't want to go back to those countries, I am proud to go. I can say to my staff that I am proud, and nothing happened to my health.

•

A busier life makes most people happier.

•

45

Does Hard Work Harm Your Family Life?

A lot of people ask me about the effect of hard work on family life. Does it have an adverse effect? I believe that a happy family life is the key to all successful accomplishments. However, most Daewoo people—myself included—believe that working diligently does not harm the family; rather, it brings fulfillment. This attitude makes us different from people in the advanced countries.

I feel that the destruction of family life occurs because of immoral conduct—when there is too much free time. I believe that a hardworking person can receive love and respect from his or her spouse and children.

Anyone who wants to be a top executive has to sacrifice something. An employee who wants more time with his or her family can reach up to manager class, but not become top executive. If you're working hard, you won't be able to spend as much time with your family, but at least your family has greater income and prestige. I don't object if a member of our group wants a normal life, but leaders don't have much free time.

Even if you're busy, you can find time to share with your family. When I was young, my wife would complain that I spent all my time working. One evening I took her to dinner and the theater. I was tired and fell asleep during the movie. She enjoyed the film, but also appreciated that I brought her even though I was so dead tired. Once there is that kind of understanding, there is no family problem. Even though I have never had a single holiday, we have a good family life.

Generally, having less work is more painful for people because we're made to do something. If someone does nothing for two or three months, it's okay. If he or she has a one-year vacation, then that's something else. In my company, I give senior executives special leave of one to two years after ten years of work. But most of them find that is too long. The wives complain they never have much time with their husbands, so I give them a year off. But then they complain that it's too much free time. A busier life makes most people happier.

You may think that I'm socially conservative, but in Korea, America, and every country, everything is based on family and morals. Still an American husband who is fifty years old or so will go abroad, meet an attractive young lady, and divorce his wife. Any executive who did that in my country would be finished. No one would respect him. Divorce is common in the United States, but I still cannot understand how readily Americans leave their families. Who's taking care of the children—the future of the country?

Sometimes I've had differences with my wife, but despite them, our love continues to grow. When there are difficulties between husband and wife, patience can bring you together again.

•

The more awards given, the better.
They lead people to even greater
heights.

•

46

The Rewards of Awards

During the early years at Daewoo, I received numerous awards, symbols of social recognition. While such awards are a form of praise, they are also a form of confinement: because of the award, because of your reputation as an award winner, and because you want to prove your award-winning capabilities, once you have received an award you have no choice but to work even harder.

That was what I did, because I did not want to betray the trust and confidence that society had placed in me. I worked twice as hard, and the Daewoo of today is the result of that. Through my experience, I have come to believe that the more awards given, the better. They lead people to greater heights.

Koreans are not very generous when it comes to applause, praise, and prizes. When I go to the United States or Europe to give a speech, I always get plenty of applause and a lot of handshakes. At times, the handshaking has taken longer than the speech itself, and sometimes I even get fan mail afterward. But if I give the same speech in Korea, there is usually no reaction at all.

When I speak abroad, I do not get all that applause because I have given a speech on the level of Abraham Lincoln's Gettysburg Address. I get it because foreigners live in a social atmosphere conducive to praising others and applauding others. Unfortunately, the social atmosphere in Korea discourages praise and applause.

People feel good even if they win a small prize. And naturally people like to hear compliments and praise. The pride involved in winning a prize stimulates you to try harder and do better.

•

Never lose your reputation. You should regard it as dearly as life.

•

Corporations have their own work to do, and should not be taking work away from smaller firms.

•

47

The One Thing You Cannot Afford to Lose

There are a number of things a person should not lose. The most important is reputation. If losing your life is personal death, then losing your reputation is social death. It is too bad if you lose money, but you can always make more—and money was made to be used anyway. But you should never lose your reputation; you should treasure it as dearly as life.

Everyone has a name and a title, and these not only represent the person, but in a sense they are that person. If someone mentions a name, you immediately think of that person—the face, the voice, the personality, the status, the background, and perhaps the person's good points and weak points. So a name is a person. If someone mentions the Roman emperor Nero, you think of all those things for which he was infamous. If someone mentions Albert Schweitzer, you immediately think of the humanitarian work he did. That goes to show you how important a name is, and you have to make sure that your name does not become an embarrassment or a source of shame.

So how do you go about keeping a good reputation and a good name? Conduct yourself according to what you are called. If you are called a teacher, you lose your reputation by not acting like a teacher. If you are called a student, then you are expected to conduct yourself like a student. Doctors, parents, religious figures, and entrepreneurs all lose their reputations when they cease to conduct themselves as such.

Each title carries with it a certain personality. You have to have certain personal rules of conduct to be called a minister or a priest, and once you violate them you open yourself to criticism. The same goes for a teacher, a student, or a businessman.

There are, however, people in the world who are rather careless about who they are. There are parents who do not deserve to be called parents. There are increasing numbers of people who besmirch the reputations of teachers and religious figures. And the same is true for some businesspeople. All of those people have misperceived the social mission that is tied to who they are.

Today there are a lot of instructors but few real teachers. That means that teachers have lost their sense of social mission. The same applies to doctors who start to tell a patient about fees before they begin treatment.

Running a corporation entails the same type of social mission. My belief is that an entrepreneur is a person who is given the mission to contribute to national development and improvement through economic activity. If I did not feel that way and thought that the mission of entrepreneurs was to improve life for themselves and their families, then I would have given up years ago.

Even if I wanted to stop working and take it easy for a while, I could not. This is because of my name and reputation. Kim Woo-Choong is a name that has become associated with work. To stop working, I fear, would be equivalent to toppling everything on which my name is built.

Although the Daewoo Group now covers a broad range of business and industrial activities, I refuse to let Daewoo participate in certain other fields of business. The first is the service sector that caters to hedonism. Services catering to merrymaking, eating, and drinking are quick, easy ways to make money, but because of our reputation I insist that we avoid such business.

The second is the import of unnecessary consumer items. Our imports are raw materials and production materials. If the issue of importing consumer goods does come up, it would depend first on evaluation of whether or not the same products are made domestically.

The third area is business that interferes with the growth of small and medium-sized enterprises. Corporations have their own work to do, and should not be taking work away from smaller firms.

All of these self-imposed business restrictions are based on the names and reputations of Kim Woo-Choong and Daewoo. And those names are very precious to me.

*If you are going to remain on top,
you have to work much harder than
those behind you—all they need to
do is imitate you to catch up.*

48

Getting Ordinary People to Do Extraordinary Things

I believe that everyone has unlimited capabilities, but they are often not tapped except in extraordinary situations.

We started our company when Korea was poor, and we worked every day from 7:00 or 8:00 in the morning until 11:00 each night. There was a consensus that we had to do this for the country, for the company, and for ourselves. We were all very proud to work long hours. This kind of consensus caused everyone to create innovations, new ideas. Even the young staff members preparing documents made unusual efforts. At that time banks paid 26 percent interest for deposits, so we always tried to get paid the day after a shipment of garments was sent. Other companies would wait until they were asked for an invoice—or were slow to prepare the documents to be submitted to the clients for payment. But I would never do that. Instead, Daewoo's staff prepared all the documents beforehand, so that we would get paid the day after every shipment. Then we would deposit that money in the bank and get high interest. Sometimes the staff would not go home, but stayed all night typing documents so they would be ready in the morning. The bank knew we were working very hard and helped us.

Despite our long hours, there were no complaints, because of the consensus. Once you get people together like that, great power can be achieved.

Later, when I started a garment factory, the marker for cutting shirts was not perfect. Japan would not give us any technology. So I went down to the factory and we worked together to improve quality. Sometimes we cried together when we could not do it. With that kind of consensus, in a very short time we could produce the right merchandise. Eventually, our garment factory's productivity was higher than that of Japanese factories. If someone is really using his or her capability, trying hard, anything is possible. This kind of history is part of our company character. Even today buyers want to visit our plant. New factories have more equipment, automation, and a good atmosphere, but still buyers want goods from our factory. This kind of spirit is continuous, even though I stopped attending to that company full-time fifteen years ago. Its productivity is the best, it has no strikes, and its employees have confidence.

If people work heart to heart, they can solve problems. The important thing for managers is knowing how to mobilize people to do this kind of work. Our shipyard, which had a lot of difficulties, increased its productivity 100 percent in a year. I went there and dealt with the workers myself. Once we had a consensus, enormous power was unleashed.

And if you're going to remain on top, you have to work that much harder. If you remain complacent, those behind you only have to imitate you to catch up to you.

Americans do this, too, though in a different way. The American way is to create something new. If I had only a little money and was starting in the United States, I'd go for a retail shop that would be open twenty-four hours a day and would provide better service than any other. Within one or two years, everyone would come to that store. With that experience, you could open other stores. Of course, you would have to train people to operate the stores, but that's easy with hard work. Everybody can do this, but hardly anyone does his or her best. If you did, your name would be established and automatically your business would grow.

Though human capability is unlimited, many people get a certain amount of money and then become lazy. My original partner in Daewoo was like that. He and I invested $5,000 each, and once the company was worth $1 million he wanted to relax and enjoy life. But now how different we are. I had to buy out his shares, which was a big burden when the company was young. Everybody has told him that he was crazy, and now he's shy about meeting me.

•

*A person's responsibility to society
increases proportionately with his
assets. Everything that we have has
come to us from and through
society.*

•

*A nation of consumers who spend
way beyond their means is a nation
in trouble.*

•

49

The Haves Are the Problem in a Consumer Society

Over the last few years, we have become comparatively prosperous in Korea. Per capita income is now more than $6,000. The streets are filled with vehicles, we have huge department stores flaunting fine goods in their windows, and foreign travel has been opened to everyone.

Unfortunately, one of the side effects of this newfound prosperity is wasteful spending, a trend that has spread through society like a communicable disease. Even though we have become more prosperous, I certainly do not think the time has come for us to be lavish.

Although the per capita income is more than $6,000, I do

not think you can say that the situation is the same as when Japan or Taiwan reached the $6,000 level. I feel that we are actually living at a per capita income level of $2,000. Considering the inflation and the appreciation of the Korean won against the dollar, our $6,000 is closer to the $2,000 level when compared to Japanese and Taiwanese standards at the time. Yet our consumption rate is keeping pace with those of Japan and Taiwan today. We are spending incredible amounts relative to the per capita income.

Everyone in Korea seems to be spending like mad, and nobody is saving, and that means trouble. So we have to curtail the spending. People have short memories, for it has not been very long since we broke the shackles of poverty. Watching this frenetic spending is like watching a child who should be learning to walk try to make a dash.

Although the Japanese live much better than Koreans do, they live modestly. Even presidents of huge corporations live in homes only 100 to 130 square meters (about 1,075 to 1,400 square feet) in area, and they have simple furniture. The chairman of the mammoth Toshiba corporation makes over 100 million yen (about $800,000) per year, yet he lives in an 83-square-meter (900-square-foot) home and spends only 150,000 yen ($1,200) per month. In contrast, there are presidents of small firms in Korea who have homes over 330 square meters (3,500 square feet) in area and who fill these homes with luxury imported furniture. The Japanese are the world's greatest savers as well. Those savings have made Japan one of the richest nations in the world today.

* * *

Overconsumption is dangerous, and it becomes a bad habit. A nation of consumers who spend way beyond their means is a nation in trouble. This applies to advanced countries like the United States, too. The danger does not come just from the waste of money. Overspending influences the collective mentality: people become less determined to work hard, and they become more concerned with the joys and thrills to be found in the present. They want to play more than they want to work, and they fall prey to the temptations of laziness and extravagance at the expense of diligence and frugality. Instead of accumulating small amounts through healthy efforts, they look for windfalls.

All of this leads to the corruption and decay of human nature and eventually of a people and a nation.

It seems that everyone is using money as if it were water. It is time we regained our senses. This extravagance borders on a mental disorder, and the ones perpetuating it are the rich. There are now families with a car for every member, while there are other families who do not have enough room to stretch out to sleep. There are people frenziedly trying to get into golf clubs, while others commit suicide out of the despair of poverty.

The wealthy should cut back on their high living. Instead of flaunting their wealth through wanton consumption, they should be sharing their wealth with the have-nots. We have to restore the ethic of public prosperity. The wealthy should help bridge the gap between the haves and the have-nots. A nation is in trouble when the wealthy assume that it is nobody's business how they spend their money.

A couple of years ago, there was a company social affair for executives and their wives, and one man's wife showed up in a mink coat. I knew for a fact that this man could not afford a mink coat for his wife with his salary. His family also had several cars. These people were obviously living way beyond their means, unless of course they had something going on the side. And since the man was working in a procurement department, many thought that his conduct was not beyond suspicion.

I could not help but feel that this extravagance could easily become a contagion among other employees, so I gave the order to have the man discreetly relieved of his position. As far as I was concerned, there was no excuse for his wife to have a mink coat. The man left the company.

A person's responsibility to society increases proportionately with his or her assets. Everything we have has come to us from and through society. This is true of possessions, of fame, and of power. And society has not given it to us for our own selfish use. Society has bestowed it on us so that we can return it to society in an appropriate manner. To put it another way, the more you have, the more frugal you should be, and the more responsibility you have to lead social trends in a healthy direction by working harder than others and by being more frugal than others.

•

Diligence in the workplace does not mean longer hours.

•

50

Is America Losing Its Pioneer Spirit?

I sometimes worry that America's pioneering spirit, its zeal for challenging the unknown, is gradually fading away.

The good life in America seems to distort the distribution of human resources. The rush of talented graduates to Wall Street, investment banks, and law offices creates a vacuum of talent in America's manufacturing industries. Without these people, how is America to improve productivity, achieve innovative management, or pursue technological development?

Diligence in the workplace does not mean longer hours. Nor does it mean working just to work. The true value of diligence in the workplace can be found in setting a clear goal, having self-confidence, and doing one's best.

With fierce international competition, it has become essential for all manufacturers to develop new technologies and provide high-quality, low-cost products as quickly as possible. In other words, a mere product itself is no longer the most powerful factor in competitiveness; competitiveness is increasingly dependent upon the ability to reduce production time. And nothing can reduce time more than hard work.

In my opinion, the decline of American competitiveness in manufacturing was due not only to the softening of the work ethic, but also to the loss of leadership in industry, leadership which was once the pride of the world.

American industry led the world in investment and technological development, increasing world demand, but it found itself competing with national industries that were once its followers. This is because the United States had lost some of its frontier spirit, which I think is its single most important strength.

Until a short time ago, when inspecting American factories, I was genuinely confident that we could continue to compete with them. It was my impression that Korean corporations were working much harder than their American counterparts. But more recently, American corporations have shown dramatic changes, so dramatic that I started to get worried.

A recent visit to an American factory near Detroit, for example, really changed my view of U.S. industry. Even though it was after ordinary working hours, over a hundred quality control circles were at the plant discussing how to make product improvements. This was inconceivable a couple of years ago.

If such changes continue to take place in American manufacturing, the United States will enter a new period of development—and regain its international competitiveness. For a nation to be prosperous, manufacturing must remain competitive, and the key to eliminating a national deficit is to eliminate protectionism and become more global. The American manufacturing sector had been losing its competitiveness, and there is a huge national debt. The way to overcome such problems is to develop new manufacturing technology rather than to put up more barriers.

I hope that American manufacturing continues to improve, because it is important for the world that the United States maintain its leadership position; this helps assure peace and stability for other countries. Leadership means you cannot afford to stop making an effort, but have to strive harder to stay on top.

So if someone asked me: Is America losing its pioneer spirit?, I would have to say no. In fact, it looks to me as if America is regaining its famous pioneer spirit.

●

Always think in terms of the partner
in a deal getting as much out of it
as you do. If you impress upon
people that they will not take a loss
by dealing with you, your business
will thrive.

●

51

Why You Cannot Profit at the Expense of Others

P
eople cannot live alone.

Each person is a part of society, and people need one another. People make society, and at the same time society makes people. The American sociologists Peter and Brigette Berger, in their book *Sociology: A Biographical Approach,* wrote about the socialization process of the individual, and how the biography of each individual is really the story of his or her relationships with other people. They discuss how socialization makes it possible for an individual to relate to other individuals, and ultimately to the entire social universe.

The meaning of life is found in altruism, not in egotism and selfishness. But we are currently facing social problems caused by people who think that they and they alone, without

---

consideration of others, are going to live well. If you have even minimal regard for others, you could never sell drugs or put hazardous materials into foodstuffs. If you are at all sensitive to the fact that there are three-generation families living in small rented single rooms, then you would not consider buying a mink coat or speculating in real estate. Such behavior comes out of a lack of regard for one's neighbors. It is both sad and an embarrassment that there are people who do live that way.

No matter what kind of work you are doing, you should not fall into this trap of selfishness. You have to go beyond personal greed and think of the public good. You always have to remember that you are not living alone, that you are always living in relationship with other people and are dependent on them in innumerable ways, many of which we just take for granted.

Living with one another goes beyond just existing with one another; it includes prospering and developing with one another, what we call "coprosperity." And that is the basis of my corporate philosophy.

Corporations, like people, should not seek their own profits at the expense of others. Of course, the basis of corporations in a capitalist system is to turn a profit, something no one can deny. At the same time, however, corporations should not be concerned with profits alone, and they should not be out to annihilate the competition. Just as the responsible individual has obligations to society, so does a corporation. Corporations are born out of society and are part of society. And when corporations trade with foreign firms or foreign nations, the same principle applies: they must think in terms of reciprocity and coprosperity. Although profit-seeking may result in some short-term benefits, it is not wise in the long run, because other firms will stop dealing with you. The relationship will end very quickly, and you will lose.

I always think in terms of the partner getting as much out of a deal as we do, because by doing so we guarantee a healthy, mutually beneficial long-term relationship. It is important to impress upon other people and other firms that they will not take a loss by dealing with you, and I have always stood by this principle. That is why, I believe, Daewoo has been able to establish such an outstanding number of joint ventures with foreign firms. The same principle has to apply to subcontractors: we always analyze the basic costs and projected profits and make sure that we split the difference with the subcontractor.

At the same time, however, you have to make sure that you are not taking a loss. Just as you look out for the other company's interests, it should be looking out for yours. This became an issue when we were taking on a seawater treatment plant project for Prudhoe Bay, Alaska.

We received the order from America's Bechtel, renowned for its advanced technology. But after deciding to give the contract to Daewoo Shipbuilding, Bechtel started changing the conditions of the contract to our disadvantage. In addition to stating that it had the right either to terminate or delay the contract at any point, it added the condition that it would pay only after it had evaluated work completed.

I found those changes in the agreement totally unacceptable, because my principle is one of equality, fairness, and reciprocity. You have to enter an agreement as equal partners. But I was not about to toss this contract out the window after we had fought so hard and so long to get it. I went to the president of Bechtel and presented my case. I told him that contracts have to be fair, and that Daewoo was based on the principle of reciprocity. I asked him if that was not the American way as well. He evidently was not very moved by my position, however, so I told him that I would have to give up the contract based on the conditions that had been presented to me. Eventually I succeeded in getting a fair contract, and we received a substantial amount of money before we actually started work.

This principle of mutual respect, fairness, and reciprocity is essential to all human relations, not just business. People have to work for one another's benefit as well as for their own. When a company does well at the expense of others, then society is in trouble.

•

As your bones become stronger,
your head should be lower.

•

52

My Eight Steps for a Full Life

A FINAL WORD TO THE WORLD'S YOUTH

1. FULFILL YOUR POTENTIAL

Youth is not just the stage of passing from childhood to adulthood, so do not think of it as just a station between stops. It is no exaggeration to say that this time of your life will determine the quality and direction of the rest of your life.

Life carries with it pluses and minuses, affirmatives and negatives, hope and despair; and how you spend your youth will determine which way you will go.

2. HAVE DREAMS

As I said earlier, history belongs to dreamers. Only nations that have people with dreams, people who try to make dreams come true, and people who share dreams can be leaders of world history.

Your dreams have to be as pure and as clear as spring water. And such dreams have to be big dreams. You have to carry the universe with you in your heart, and your dreams have to be as big as the universe itself. A philosopher once said that youth without dreams is the same as psychological suicide. So dream dreams that are pure and bright and big.

3. THINK CREATIVELY

History is led by creative thinkers and creative people. A society that appreciates creativity and productivity will never fail. You possess the power of positive thinking, so you should always begin things affirmatively, positively. By doing so, you will lead the way.

4. CHALLENGE

History progresses through challenge and courage. People who challenge become successful. Youth likes adventure and doesn't fear failure. A person who begins things with fear has already lost his or her youth. You should burn with the fire of accomplishment. Continuously develop yourself and strive for greater heights in order to satisfy such desires for accomplishment.

5. SACRIFICE

History grows on sacrifice. One generation must sacrifice for the following generation to prosper.

6. BE ALTRUISTIC

People are made to live together; no one lives alone. Egocentrism is no good, so you must not be polluted by the biases of egocentricity and personal greed. Think of the group before yourself, and consider the public good before personal profit. Do not become polluted by egotism and personal greed. Head into tomorrow together with faith and love.

7. BE TRUE TO YOURSELF

No matter how hard my generation may have tried to be true to ourselves, it was difficult because of family or work obligations. At times, we were forced by situations to say and do things that we did not want to. But you do not have to face that. Be sure that you do not become entrapped or snared in chains. Consider going after what you really want as the greatest way of being true to yourself.

8. BE MODEST

Growth and development come from learning. Growth stops the minute you think you are really important, when you think you know something. Growth and development come from humbling yourself and striving to learn as much as you can.

As your bones become stronger, your head should be

lower. We have so much to learn from the beads of sweat on a farmer's brow, from the oil on a factory worker's overalls, from the warm touch of a parent preparing breakfast in pre-dawn darkness. Open your eyes and ears to the sights and sounds around you, humble yourself, and study hard.